BERLI

G000088430

GREEK ISLANDS

- A  in the text denotes a highly recommended sight
- A complete A–Z of practical information starts on p.115
- Extensive mapping throughout: on cover flaps and in text

Copyright © **1996** by Berlitz Publishing Co. Ltd, Berlitz House, Peterley
Road, Oxford OX4 2TX, England, and Berlitz Publishing Company,
Inc., 257 Park Avenue South, New York, NY 10010, USA.

All rights reserved. No part of this book may be reproduced or
transmitted in any form or by any means, electronic or mechanical,
including photocopying, recording or by any information storage and
retrieval system without permission in writing from the publisher.

Berlitz Trademark Reg. US Patent Office and other countries.

Marca Registrada.

Printed in Switzerland by Weber SA, Bienne.

18th edition (1996/1997)

**Although we make every effort to ensure the accuracy of the
information in this guide, changes do occur. If you have any
new information, suggestions or corrections to contribute, we
would like to hear from you. Please write to Berlitz Publishing
at one of the above addresses.**

Text:	Jack Altman
Editors:	Donald Greig, Peter Duncan
Photography:	Pete Bennett
Layout:	Suzanna Boyle
Cartography:	Visual Image
Thanks to:	Miki Benaki for his invaluable assistance in the preparation of this guide. Thanks also to Paris Tselios.

Front cover: *Ia Town, Santorini, The Cyclades*

p.4 photograph: *Skiathos harbour, The Cyclades*

CONTENTS

The Islands and the Islanders

The Greek islands have always occupied a special place in the hearts of this seafaring nation. This has held since those days when Odysseus island-hopped his way home from the Trojan Wars, right up to the modern era of shipping magnates, bred most frequently on Aegean islands like Chios and Andros.

In attempts to sort out the country's myriad isles, islets, rocky outcrops and sandbars, geographers argue about just how many proper islands there are. Officially they are numbered at 1,425, of which only 169 are inhabited – most of those more by goats and sheep than by humans. The largest islands are Crete and Evia, the latter linked by a bridge to the mainland northeast of Athens. The remainder generally form distinct archipelagos.

The most accessible islands from Athens are the Cyclades, spilling down into the central and southern Aegean to form a kind of circle, as their Greek name suggests, with the venerable sanctuary-island of Delos at its centre. The most popular of the Cyclades are Mykonos and Santorini (also known as Thera). Across the Aegean to the southeast, the Dodecanese comprise a dozen islands close by the Turkish coast. Besides the principal island of Rhodes, the best known are Kos and Patmos. The main grouping of Sporades, literally a 'scattering' of islands, is located north of Evia and includes Skiathos and Skopelos. In the eastern Aegean another group consists of Chios, Lesvos and Samos, while in the northern Aegean, closer to the northern mainland, lies a further collection embracing Thasos, Samothraki and Limnos.

The Aegean Sea is an arm of the Mediterranean. It measures about 640km (400 miles) longitudinally, from the north Greek coast of Thrace to its southern limits at Rhodes and Crete. Across, from the Greek to the Turkish coasts, it spans 320km (200 miles). Most of **5** the islands' terrain is mountainous and arid, with few if any rivers, and only a tiny part of the land is arable. Nevertheless, the Aegean also furnishes Greece's popular, travel-poster image of dazzling white houses and churches set around a small harbour, as on Mykonos

A Mykonos fisherman ponders his catch (below); a dreamy day ends over Santorini (right).

or Sifnos in the Cyclades, or up on the cliffs of Santorini further south.

Greek holidaymakers – the Greeks take holidays, too – are often puzzled by the northern European taste for these islands' craggy landscape. They prefer to head for the greener islands of Andros or Paros in the Cyclades, or further north to Thasos. In the Dodecanese islands of the eastern Aegean, the old charms of Kos are becoming less easy to enjoy in high season, while attractive Skiathos in the Sporades is threatened with a similar fate.

On these islands in particular, the tourist industry – now an essential mainstay of not just the local, but the national economy as well – has driven many of the island's peasants and fishermen into the sale of souvenirs and the restaurant business (or to a new life in the mainland cities). On the characterful islands, however, like Tinos in the Cyclades, Poros off the Peloponnese or Chios close by the Turkish coast, the local population has remained firmly entrenched.

Black or White

The tale of how the Aegean Sea got its name is a sad one. Aegeus was the loving father of the legendary hero Theseus, who had crossed the sea to Crete to slay the dreaded Minotaur. It had been agreed that if Theseus survived his fight with the monster – a creature half-bull, half-man – the returning fleet's black sails would be changed to white. The lad triumphed over the Minotaur but forgot to change the sails. From a look-out on the mainland, old Aegeus saw the black sails of death returning and killed himself in despair. He was accorded the posthumous honour of bequeathing his name to the sea.

After 400 years of domination by the Ottoman Empire, the Turkish influence is still visible and it would be fruitless to deny it, though it is often too sensitive a point to be raised in public. Nearly all the mosques and other public buildings of distinctly Turkish origin (like bathhouses) have been destroyed and the place names Hellenicized, but there remain nonetheless certain aspects of Greek life with Turkish connections that can hardly be ignored. The uniform of the presidential palace guard in Athens, for instance, although modelled on the heroic rebels of 1821 (see p.22), looks un-

commonly 'Turkish'. With regard to local cuisine, especially yoghurt dishes and honeyed desserts, it is not clear how much is truly of Turkish origin or merely appropriated by the conquerors from Greece itself. Greek *ouzo* and Turkish *raki* are close cousins, and while it **7** may not be a good idea to order 'Turkish' coffee, you'll find that the Greek equivalent, *ellinikos*, is much the same.

So what in particular makes a modern Greek? Just as ancient Greece spread its culture throughout the Mediterranean, so their neighbours returned the compliment by invasion or peaceful commerce. Too many Persians, Phoenicians, Egyptians, Serbs, Turks, Albanians and Italians have passed this way and lingered for it to be credible that Greeks bear any resemblance now to their ancestors of antiquity. In this respect it is worth noting that, despite the wealth of classical sculpture, we have no definite idea of what ancient Greeks looked like, for the representation of male and female figures in art reflected an artistic ideal rather than biological reality.

The swarthy inhabitants of today, flashing eyed and strong nosed, may seem to have the country's dramatic landscape etched in their faces. In temperament, the islanders tend to be somewhat calmer than their volatile and excitable cousins

Colours are more brilliant in the Cycladic sun; here the cats set the tone for the sacred siesta.

on the mainland, and in another sense more sombre.

Almost a group apart are the returning *imigrés*, who are regarded with a mixture of envy and admiration for their Mercedes from Stuttgart or Chevrolet from Detroit. The idea of 'emigration' is an old Greek phenomenon dating from the time when Spartans, Corinthians and a mixture of Aegean islanders founded colonies all around the Mediterranean. In the words of the great historian Herodotus, they sat there 'like frogs around a pond', only returning from time to time to the homeland to show off their new-found wealth and knowledge. Since the 1970s the *imigrés* have been coming back to their country in ever-increasing numbers, bringing a welcome fund of intellectual and industrial experience – not to mention hard currency. Many

8

return just to retire to the ancestral home town, where they build palatial, though not always very handsome houses, which change the face of traditional communities.

Whatever conflicts of interest may appear, the men give free rein to their passions at the all important café conversations. Here you can see how natural it was for this fiercely independent people, ever sceptical of authority, to lay the foundations of democracy – even if it has been a struggle ever since to keep it going. The general taste for democracy is tempered – though not necessarily contradicted – by a preference for strong, almost patriarchal leadership. In those endless debates around café tables, one man always seems to exert a natural though sometimes spurious authority. He leans back in his chair, speaks loudly, leads – and stops – the **9**

In this house on Delos, the patricians have lost their heads but not their elegance.

laughter, mostly ignoring any remarks that are not affirmations of what he has just said. He can usually be recognized by his distinctive hat, walking stick and thick wad of notes with which he pays the bill.

The local Orthodox priest also plays a prominent role at the café table, smoking, drinking coffee, dispensing advice, listening to local gossip, arbitrating or at least halting heat-

ed arguments. The reverence paid to him by the local community dates in part from the time of the Turks, when priests enjoyed a privileged political position in society. Getting on the ferry, people rush to pay his fare or help him with his bags, even when he is young enough to handle them himself, and often younger than his helpful parishioner.

On the rare occasions when they attend, the older women observe their men with a certain amused detachment. More often, however, they gather on balconies or around the market stalls to discuss the vital business of match-making and -unmaking. Younger girls are not so different from their European counterparts, though still perhaps a little more demure.

Greeks are usually amazed and delighted to discover any foreigner speaking their language. They frequently manage a little English, German, French or Italian, roughly in that order, but will immediately be well disposed to you if you try at least a few Greek words as a sign of good intent.

A simple *parakalò* ('please') or *efkaristò* ('thank you') goes a long way, as does *kaliméra* ('good morning') or *kalispéra* ('good evening'). This is very much a place where the effort to get underneath the tourist surface pays huge dividends. The Greek islands are certainly a paradise of beaches and sunsets, antiquities and luxuries, but now more than ever

before, what makes them so unique is the local people. All that remains to be said is: *Kalò taksidhi* – 'Bon voyage!

(As major Aegean destinations, CRETE and RHODES each have separate Berlitz Pocket Guides, as does CORFU among the Ionian Islands of the Adriatic. The group of Saronic Islands is covered in the Berlitz ATHENS Pocket Guide.)

The Name Game

There is no fast rule for Roman-lettered versions of Greek place names on signposts and road maps. You should have no problem recognizing that *Limnos* and *Lemnos* or even *Hios* and *Chios* are the same place, but watch out with *Santorini*: Greeks shun the Italianate name for their own *Thera* or *Thira*. Some also shy away from *Lesvos* (or *Lesbos*), preferring *Mytilene*. The main town on each island, which generally shares the island's name (eg *Samos* or *Mykonos*), may be known as *Hora* or *Chora* (simply meaning 'town') or, if it is also a port, *Skala*.

The names used in this guide are those most generally accepted in western Europe, with bracketed mentions of variations and transcriptions of Greek alternatives.

Finding your way around the towns will be much easier if you familiarize yourself with the Greek alphabet (see p.128). Two things to remember: all street signs are written in capital letters, and the words for street (*odos*) and square (*plateia*) are used in conversation but usually omitted from maps and signs.

A Brief History

The scattering of all those islands right across the Aegean served as a marvellous incentive to prehistoric men to expand their horizons. Instead of staying put in their caves on the cliffside, whether on the Greek mainland or on what are now the Turkish coasts of Asia Minor, they could look across to the nearest island and set off to find out what was there. Instead of the flimsy craft they used for offshore fishing, they had to construct more sturdy vessels that could weather the longer distances. It was almost certainly this tantalizing challenge of island-hopping that prompted European development of open sea navigation.

The most enterprising of the earliest sailors to explore these uninhabited islands, approximately 9,000 years ago, were the Phoenicians, who first settled all along the Aegean's east coastline (before limiting their territory to the Lebanon and

Ariadne on Naxos

Supremacy in the Aegean was a constant bone of contention between Athens and Crete, and in ancient legend this conflict was symbolized by Crete's Minotaur monster devouring 14 Athenian boys and girls every nine years.

One of the victims, Theseus, put a stop to it with the aid of Ariadne, the daughter of King Minos of Crete. Theseus slew the Minotaur, seduced Ariadne, and took her with him when he left Crete. On the journey back to Athens, the ship put in at Naxos, where Theseus abandoned Ariadne, now pregnant.

Stranded on Naxos, Ariadne married Dionysus, god of wine and became a fertility goddess – 'fruitful mother of the barley'. She bore Dionysus six children, among them the hot-blooded Phaedra, who eventually had the gall to marry Theseus herself.

Palestine). Although they established small colonies on the north eastern islands of Thasos and Samothraki (Samothrace), the Phoenicians – always consummate merchants – were at first less interested in settlement than in exploiting the islands' resources for trade.

Early Settlements in the Cyclades

On the island of Milos in the Cyclades, east of the Peloponnese, the Phoenicians discovered plentiful supplies of high grade obsidian, a hard glassy volcanic rock used before the Bronze Age in manufacturing knives and razors. Through the spread of these ancient implements and other manufactured goods from the Levant, today's archaeologists have traced the movement of the Phoenicians across the Aegean. Their new sails and multiple systems of oarsmen carried Aegean products as far as southern France and Spain.

After a while, the merchants were accompanied or followed by farmers and fishermen who

Ancient ritual on Delos, principal religious centre and treasury for the Aegean islands.

settled in Crete and also, by 4000 BC, in the Cyclades. A flourishing civilization developed as the island craftsmen worked in stone, clay, obsidian, then lead, bronze and other metals, refining the techniques which had originated in the Levant. Early Cycladic sculpture was most notable for its **13** distinctive marble statuettes in the forms of goddesses, harp-players and other musicians.

With the gradual dawning of the Bronze Age after 2700 BC, new arrivals from what is now western Turkey introduced a variety of bronze weaponry, defensive fortifications and the Mesopotamian pottery wheel to step up their production in ceramics. Prosperity grew with trade in Milos obsidian, white marble from Paros and grey marble from Naxos, and the islands' artisans spread the influence of Cycladic culture to the more primitive mainland.

Minoan Civilization

Around 2000 BC, most of the Aegean islands fell under the influence of Crete's flourishing Minoan kingdom. The southernmost and largest of Greek islands created a maritime empire not by military conquest, but by the material appeal of its highly colourful culture. Its northern neighbour, Santorini (Thera to ancient and modern Greeks), played a leading role in that empire, and boasted a society which was probably as rich and sophisticated as that of Knossos itself. On Santorini's southern peninsula, just 112km (70 miles) from Crete, archaeologists have only recently discovered magnificent Minoan-style frescoes, sculpture and pottery, and imposing remains of ashlar stone houses with elaborate plumbing and central heating. These, along with Crete's own palaces, were buried under lava and cinders by the massive volcanic eruptions and earthquakes which shook the region in 1500 BC, undoubtedly the greatest natural disaster in antiquity. The cataclysm ended Crete's empire in the Aegean.

Mycenaeans, Dorians and Phoenicians

By 1300 BC, Mycenaeans operating from fortified strongholds along the Peloponnese mainland had become the preeminent power in the area, this time not mercantile but strictly military. Their belligerent exploits, as later chronicled by Homer in both *The Iliad* and

The Odyssey, led them under King Agamemnon across the Aegean to Troy on the coast of Asia Minor, picking up mercenaries from islands on the way.

The Mycenaeans were in due course conquered by 'barbarians', more recently identified as Dorians from northern and eastern Europe. The Dorians' war machine brought iron to Greece around 1100 BC, but their arrival heralded a decline in written records and the fine arts, and the next two or three chaotic centuries came to be known as the Dark Age.

The Dorians and colonists from Asia Minor settled on the rim of the Aegean and some of the islands, while the Phoenicians moved in to control the profitable sea-trading routes. From this fusion of peoples a unifying alphabet developed for a Greek language, influenced principally by Phoenician and Hebrew, and with it, a

The Romans built this Odeon amphitheatre on Kos, a popular spa resort during classical times.

specifically Greek civilization began to assert itself during the 8th century BC. From about the time of the first Olympic Games in 776 BC, the Greeks embarked on an unprecedented wave of expansion. Aegean islands contributed settlers to nearly 200 colonies formed in and around the Black Sea and Mediterranean. Typically, survivors from volcano-devastated Thera crossed to the North African coast to found the prosperous colony of Cyrene in what is now Libya.

Homer probably wrote his epics on the island of Chios around the end of the 8th century BC, while nearby Lesvos was home to three outstanding 7th-century lyric poets – Terpander, Sappho and Alcaeus – and the island of Paros honoured the poet Archilochos for his elegiac verse. Naxos was the main political and economic power. Samos, flourishing during the 6th century under the tyrant Polycrates, boasted the largest temple of the age in its enormous sanctuary for the

How Many Homers?

It is still not clear whether Homer was one man or two, but with all that insider knowledge of seafaring in *The Odyssey*, scholars are convinced that at least one of them was an islander. Supporters of the two-Homers theory, for complex textual reasons, suggest that the *Iliad* was composed by a poet from Anatolia (perhaps from Smyrna, now Izmir in western Turkey) and the *Odyssey* by an inhabitant of Chios.

All we can surmise of Homer the man, judging from his sympathy for the common peasant, is that he was probably himself of humble peasant origin. Was he blind, as imaginary sculptures often show him? Greek bards often were. It has been suggested that blindness would have been an asset in memorizing without distraction the long poems they recited at royal courts.

goddess Hera. Centre of religious worship in the Aegean was the small Cycladic island of Delos, revered as Apollo's birthplace. By organizing the purification of Apollo's sanctuary – no births or burials allowed on the island – Athens' rulers imposed their authority over the Cyclades. Their control over the Aegean was expanded by the end of the 6th century with the founding of overseas colonies in the north.

The Persian Wars

By the 6th century BC, the Persians had emerged as the main threat to Athenian supremacy in the Aegean. From a controlling position on the Anatolian coast, they converted northern and eastern islands into Persian satrapies (in ancient Persia a satrap was a provincial governor), notably Samos and Chios. To the south, the wealth and strength of Naxos attracted their attention in 499 BC. A first bold Persian attack was beaten off, but nine years later a fleet carrying 25,000 men swept back over the Cyclades.

These invaders occupied but spared Delos, while burning Naxos to the ground.

After a glorious mainland victory at Marathon, the Greek forces regained control of the sea in the battle of Salamis (480 BC), with various ships of Athens' Aegean island-allies playing a key role. Samos was forced to fight on the Persian side; some islands like Andros and Paros contributed ships to the Persian fleet for mercenary gain – and were duly punished by Athens after the wars.

Athens, by then the most powerful of the mainland city-states, enlisted the islands and some other Greek supporters into the Delian League, named after Delos where the common treasury was kept (the 'Brussels' of a NATO-like alliance). Samos, Chios, and Lesvos all contributed ships, while other members paid annual tribute. In effect the League became the Athenian empire, controlling the islands for most of the 5th century. At various times Naxos, Thasos and Lesvos fell out with Athens but were prevented from actually leaving **17**

*S*t John wrote his Revelations on Patmos (above); a mosaic in Chios monastery (right).

the alliance. In 454 BC the regular treasury contributions of the Aegean islands were transferred to Athens, where Pericles used them to finance some of the most glorious constructions of the classical age.

The islands escaped most of the bloodshed of the painfully protracted Peloponnesian War (431-404 BC) between Athens and Sparta. Individual islands played off one power against the other, most of them deserting Athens when Sparta's final victory seemed imminent. In time, they found themselves subject – along with the rest of Greece – to Philip II of Macedonia and his son Alexander the Great, who succeeded to the throne in 336 BC.

The Roman Empire

The Hellenistic Period which followed saw Delos prosper again for about 150 years as a free port and key trading centre. During the 2nd century BC, Rhodes prevailed over many

Aegean islands. Apart from a brief incursion by the Black Sea forces of Mithridates running over the Greek islands and mainland in 88 BC, the entire Greek world was incorporated into the Roman Empire by the the first century BC. For approximately 400 years, the Romans ruled pagan Greece, while Christianity struggled to take root. Patmos achieved a revered reputation in Christian history as the site where, in about AD 95, St John wrote the Book of Revelation. It wasn't until AD 330, however, when the newly converted Emperor Constantine made Byzantium, as Constantinople, capital of his Eastern Empire, that Christianity was assured of its dominant role in future Greek life.

The Byzantine Period

The islands were at first spared the invasions in the 6th century by Slav, Avar, Hun and Bulgar hordes, but in AD 623, a new wave of Slavs plundered their way south to Crete. Thereafter the hapless islanders were further weakened by epidemics and forced drafts for Byzantine wars against the Arabs. In the 9th century, the Moslem forces wrought havoc around the undefended Aegean. When at last Emperor Nicephorus recovered the islands (961-965) they were almost depopulated.

After the Crusaders (transported on Venetian ships) captured Constantinople in 1204, the Aegean islands were divided up among other Byzantine spoils. Venice occupied Crete and turned over the minor islands to Italian adventurers, who founded family dynasties

on them. The most important was the so-called Duchy of the Archipelago, which was controlled by Marco Sanudo and his successors on Naxos. For a time, the Genoese stepped in to contest rule for commercially lucrative islands, in particular Chios and Lesvos, both attractive posts for trade with Black Sea and Asia Minor.

Coming of the Turks

Late in the 13th century the Ottoman Turks made their first appearance, raiding islands in the eastern Aegean. This new power was on the rise, though Western influence remained in place and was not eliminated for a long time even after the Turks took Constantinople and the Byzantine Empire in 1453.

In 1309, the Knights of St John took over control of the Dodecanese from their citadel on Rhodes. They withstood a Turkish siege during 1480, but were displaced in 1522. The Genoese, after losing Chios to Greek nationalists, returned in 1329 to hold the island until finally expelled by the Turks in

1566. On the Cycladic islands of Tinos, Mykonos and Andros, the Venetians maintained important positions well into the 16th and 17th centuries.

During the 16th century, the Aegean became the focal point of a lively black market in grain, with Greek ships repeatedly evading Turkey's ban on shipments to the west. British and Italian adventurers were forever carrying off precious marble antiquities for wealthy patrons back home – many are now displayed in the museums of Oxford, London and Rome.

In 1770 Russia declared war on Turkey and Catherine the Great sent her fleet to help the Greeks win back the Peloponnese. When the mission failed, the Russians captured instead over a dozen islands, including Naxos, which remained under their control until 1774. The expedition was led by Catherine's lover, Alexei Orlov, who between island-grabbing had the gall to write: 'The natives here are sycophantic, deceitful, impudent, fickle and cowardly, completely given over to money and plunder.'

HISTORICAL LANDMARKS

7000 BC Phoenicians explore Aegean islands.

2000 BC Aegean dominated commercially by Minoan Crete.

1500 BC Earthquakes herald end of Minoan civilization.

1100-900 BC Dorian invasions mark start of Dark Age.

8th century BC Greek culture develops; Homer writes *Iliad*.

6th-5th century BC Persian invasions, culminating in their defeat by Greeks at Salamis in 480 BC – islands playing key role.

431-404 BC Sparta defeats Athens in Peloponnesian War.

336 BC Alexander the Great rules Greek empire.

31 BC Roman Empire completes annexation of Greek territories.

AD 95 St John writes *Book of Revelation* on Patmos.

9th-10th century Islands under Moslem attack; population falls.

1204 Crusaders seize Constantinople, Venice colonizes Cyclades and Crete, Genoese contest for rule of Chios and Lesvos.

13th century First raids by Ottoman Turks in Eastern Aegean.

1309 Knights of St John begin rule of Dodecanese from Rhodes.

1522 Ottoman Turks expel Knights of St John from Dodecanese.

1566 Genoese driven from Chios by Ottoman Turks.

1770-1774 Russian occupation of over 12 Aegean islands.

1821-1822 War of Independence crushed by Turks.

1832 Cyclades among first islands included in Greek kingdom.

1912 Treaty of Lausanne transfers Dodecanese to Italy, as trustee.

1913 Northern and eastern Aegean islands become Greek.

1939-1944 During World War II, combined Greek and Allied forces relinquish control of southern Aegean to Germans.

1944-1949 Civil war in Greece – largely bypassing islands.

1967-1974 Dictatorship of the Colonels; massive emigration.

1982 Greece joins the European Union (formerly 'Community').

1994 Dispute with Turkey over rights for Aegean oil and fisheries. **21**

Towards Greek Independence

In Greece's bitter struggle for liberation from four centuries of Turkish domination, the islanders of the Aegean played a colourful role. After centuries of treading a fine line between commerce and piracy, the brigands of the high seas lent their bloody talents to the nationalist cause. Islands in the eastern Aegean like Lesvos and Chios controlled sea lanes, often delaying or preventing supplies from getting through to the Turks, while others sustained insurgent Greek coastal ports. Samos in particular won such a reputation that for the Turks the phrase 'to go to Samos' became synonymous with certain death. In 1822 the Turks put down the revolt – brutally on Chios and nearby Psara, where they killed 25,000 people and enslaved nearly twice as many.

When independence was finally achieved in 1832 and the great powers chose the teenage Bavarian Prince Otto to be the first king of Greece, only the Cyclades and a few other islands were initially included in the territory of the new nation.

The 20th Century

With the Treaty of Lausanne of 1912, Turkey transferred the Dodecanese islands over to the Italians, ostensibly in trust for eventual union with Greece.

Turbaned Moslem tombs are a reminder of the turbulent Turkish presence on the island of Chios.

This was not such a bad thing as people have since claimed. The Italians did at least embark on an ambitious public building and roads programme to remedy the dereliction of the stagnant Ottoman regime. Crete, the eastern islands of Samos, Chios and Lesvos, and the northern Aegean islands of Limnos, Thasos and Samothraki only became Greek after the end of the Balkan Wars.

Greece tried to stay neutral during World War II. However, Mussolini (who had by then seized Albania) cherished the ambition of adding the rest of the country to his *de facto* possession of the Dodecanese islands as part of a new Italian empire in the Mediterranean. The initial Italian attack, when it came in October 1940, was decisively repulsed, but it was followed by a fierce German onslaught six months later.

British, Australian and New Zealand forces joined Greek forces, but the Germans forced their opponents to withdraw to Crete and, in a costly airborne operation, took possession of that island, too, in June 1941.

They controlled the southern Aegean from bases in Crete and Rhodes. Samos was badly bombed by the Germans, and their Bulgarian ally occupied Samothraki and Thasos.

Even before the end of the war in 1945, Greece was experiencing internal strife among communists, royalists and others on the extreme right. The ensuing civil war largely bypassed the islands, but Samos was beset by fierce fighting.

It took Greece some time to recover from a decade at war, and previous bitternesses were not easily forgotten. Between 1967 and 1974 the country fell under the repressive military dictatorship of the 'Colonels'.

In recent years large subsidies from the European Union (formerly European Community), which Greece joined in 1982, have again brought the prospect of prosperity to the Aegean. In 1994, the Aegean became an area of dispute between Greece and Turkey, this time over territorial claims to rights for oil-prospecting and fishing, but the flow of tourists continues unabated.

23

Where to Go

Deciding on where to go in the Aegean islands and how to set about it usually depends on the relative importance you attach to the three basic reasons for heading there in the first place: soaking up the sun and the sea; visiting the ancient and Byzantine monuments; or getting to know the people and the land itself. Some visitors plump for one at the expense of the other two. To enjoy the islands to the full, we would recommend a combination of all three. That way, you're likely to go home a little browner (these days, don't overdo it), a little wiser and much more cheerful.

We have divided the region into five groups of islands. If you imagine the adventure of an odyssey around the entire Aegean, the arrangement describes a wide loop from the Cyclades, south east to the Dodecanese (excluding Rhodes), up to the East Aegean islands of Samos, Chios and Lesvos, on to Limnos, Samothraki and Thasos in the North Aegean, and ending with the western Sporades – Skiathos, Alonissos and Skopelos.

However austere you may imagine archaeological ruins to be, the monumental sites like the sanctuary of Delos or ancient city of Thera on Santorini exert a mysterious power on the most blasé imagination. Quite apart from the mystic attractions of Byzantine churches and their icons, the moment of meditation they allow can be cooling for body and spirit alike. Taken in small doses before the heat of the day, the ancient or medieval monuments may act as a tonic stimulus if sun bathing threatens to addle your brain. One of the best things about Mykonos, for instance, is its easy accessibility to the Delos sanctuary – even the most hardened beach addict can visit the ruins in the morning and be back building sand replicas in the afternoon.

If you want to avoid the most crowded islands popularized by package tours, you can still find more secluded spots, but hotel accommodation and general tourist facilities will be correspondingly more modest. The answer here is to rent a house and 'go native'.

WHEN TO GO

The Aegean has a relatively short spring, sweltering summer, cooler autumn and a winter which might well be mild in temperature but which often feels wretchedly cold. Summers are slightly cooler on the islands, but also stickier at night. The rains come mainly in April and October.

From time to time between mid-July and the end of August, the sultry face of summer is buffeted by the notorious *meltemi* wind. Stirred up by a collision of sharply differing pressure systems between the Balkans and North Africa, this northwest wind sets in around 8am and peters out at sunset. Beach umbrellas take off and windsurfers fly across the sea.

Wherever you find yourself in summer, one institution remains sacred – the siesta. Between 3 and 5 in the afternoon, all but the most diligent, yuppified Greeks are busy resting. Don't phone them. Don't try to beat them, join them.

High volume tourist traffic can make travelling difficult at certain times in the high season. May, June and September are the most attractive months for easy movement around the popular destinations.

Time out from an extraordinary morning's sightseeing on Delos, somewhere on Mount Kynthos.

The Cyclades

Scattered across the southern Aegean east of Athens and the Attic peninsula, the leisurely Cyclades encourage a carefree way of life among easy-going islanders who refuse to be hurried. The islands are first port of call for those chasing the Greek holiday dream: here you can spend lazy mornings at a harbour overlooked by blue-doored, brilliant white houses and chapels; enjoy a few hours on the best of the Aegean's beaches; dip into a little culture if the notion takes you; and round it all off with some lively nightlife.

The name of the archipelago comes from the circle (*cyclos*) which a dozen islands form around the sanctuary of Delos, birthplace of Apollo. In modern times, the group has been extended to include another 20 islands as far south as Santorini (slowly resuming its ancient name of Thera). The modern administrative capital is Siros, an industrialized island west of Mykonos involved in cotton and tanning.

Cypresses and olive groves, orange and lemon trees blossoming beautifully in spring lend their colour to the largely arid brown landscapes. Settlers have added dovecotes, windmills and now-ruined castles.

Their all too obvious attractions have made many of the

*T*he pride of a man and his mule on their way to market at Mykonos Town.

Cyclades prey to the package tour trade. Secluded corners remain to be discovered, however, and the charms of the popular islands, like Mykonos and Santorini, are powerful enough to withstand the commercial onslaught – even with the summer *meltemi* wind at its strongest in this south west corner of the Aegean.

MYKONOS

The miracle of Mykonos is that it still manages to live up to the expectations of those who want the perfect hedonistic holiday. It attracts everyone from the smart yachting fraternity to the most modest backpackers, as well as lovers of classical Greece who come for its easy access to the Delos island sanctuary. Many of the island's permanent residents are expatriate artists, writers and cheerful replicas of the hippies who flocked here in the 1960s. Mykonos' old reputation for sexual freedom has been tempered by a more recent prudence, but nude beaches still abound on the island.

*T*he simple beauty of a red-roofed church in the drowsy inland town of Ano Mera.

The canny visitor will find antidotes to the island's more commercial aspect. For every crowded beach within easy access of Mykonos Town, another off the beaten track offers peace and splendid swimming, accessible to any enterprising visitor by boat or motor-scooter. (When renting a car here, make sure it has four-wheel-drive for the many unpaved roads down to the beaches.) If the main town centre is indeed **27** chock-a-block with boutiques, bars and restaurants, a brief tour will reveal that they are bright and not tawdry, selling good quality merchandise. The locally handwoven linen is especially fine. With the cruise traffic in mind, the tone is definitely 'upmarket'. The island's trump card has been to avoid hideous jerry-built blockhouses through strict enforcement of a traditional-architecture ordinance, so that even its most recent hotels may look like a series of fishermen's cottages.

The islanders themselves remain (diplomatically) friendly and have overcome a tendency to baldness noticed by Strabo, Greek geographer of the 1st century BC. However, the landscape of the interior is as barren as ever.

Mykonos Town

Surrounded by low hills on the west side of the island, the principal town hugs its harbour in an embrace of narrow winding lanes and alleys deliberately laid out as a labyrinth to confuse medieval pirates.

Three landmark windmills loom above the **port**, at its best during early morning and late afternoon, outside the shore-leave hours of the cruise passengers. Small boats handling the Delos excursion traffic are moored along the natural jetty of the harbour's north arm. Bigger boats dock round to the east. The quay is shared by cafés, fishermen and an occasional tame pelican, a languid island mascot since the languid hippie 60s. With water often lapping right below their portside windows, the delightful balconied houses of the **Alefkandra quarter** have encouraged the nickname of 'Little Venice' for this area.

Above the port, the spotlessly whitewashed **Paraportiani church**, more backdrop than building, seems to be held in greater reverence by hordes of pagan photographers than devout Christians.

The small **Archaeological Museum** out at Agios Stefanos in the north is devoted principally to tomb sculpture and ceramics from the Rhenia cemetery, where the dead of

CYCLADES HIGHLIGHTS

The unpredictable state of Greek opening hours is fully covered on p.132. Here we just give you the location of the more important museums and archaeological sites, but inquire at the tourist office for up-to-date information about access.

Mykonos: culturally better known for nightlife than museums, but the little Archaeological Museum at Agios Stefanos is worth a look. *Beaches*: nudists can officially go to Paradise and Super-Paradise on Karkingari Bay (unofficially almost anywhere); chic crowds go to Elia; water sports enthusiasts head for Panormos Bay. (See p.31)

Delos: Sanctuary of Apollo, central shrine of Aegean in classical Greece, should not be missed and can be reached from Mykonos, Tinos, Naxos or Paros. (See p.33)

Andros: for a change of pace from ever-present art of ancient Greece, explore Andros Town's Museum of Modern Art. (See p.37)

Sifnos: interesting pottery workshops in port of Kamares. *Beaches*: Platis Gialos is for families, remote Vathi Bay for lovers. (See p.40)

Paros: above classical white Cycladic houses of Parikia, see Kastro, hilltop Venetian citadel, and Archaeological Museum near cathedral; most attractive villages: fishing port of Naoussa and Lefkes in the mountains. *Beaches*: make your sand-pies at Kolibithres and Drios, windsurf at Piso Livadi, go out to Antiparos for snorkelling and cave-exploring. (See p.42)

Naxos: good icons in Panagia Theoskepastos church and Catholic Cathedral. *Beaches*: Lionas' marble pebbles ideal on windy days, Agios Prokopios offers sand and seclusion. (See p.45)

Santorini: Fira Town features fine jewellery shops, charming hangout at nearby fishing harbour of Ia; visit Profitis Ilias Monastery and archaeological sites at Akrotiri and Ancient Thera. *Beaches*: spectacular black volcanic sand at Perissa, pebbles at Kamari welcome on windy days, romantic trysts out at Monolithos. (See p.51)

Ios: all-day party time in Ios Town. *Beaches*: busiest at Milopotamos, access by boat thins out crowds at beaches around Manganari Bay, sexiest goings-on at Agios Theodotis. (See p.51)

Delos were buried after the sanctuary's purification in the 5th century BC. Most notable are a statue of Hercules and a fine 7th-century-BC *pitho*s or jar decorated with scenes from the Trojan War.

Beaches

The island boasts more than a dozen above-standard beaches, but unless you like the bustle of a crowded beach, the best are the remotest on the north coast or at the east end of the island. As you hunt down your ideal location, remember that on an island where winds often blow up in the summer without warning, fine-sand beaches can prove more irksome than those with pebbles or coarse-grained sand.

Closest to town and all accessible by road are **Ornos**, **Tourlos** and **Agios Stefanos**. Almost as convenient – just an inexpensive 15-minute taxi or bus ride from town – but extremely crowded are **Psarou** and **Platis Gialos**. These are

more conventional than the secluded coves and beaches further along the coast, where people become inclined to ignore the threat of the amusing English sign: 'Is forbidden for the undressed people in order of the police'.

While waiting for your spiny lobster (above) gaze out at the old windmills of Mykonos.

Paranga and the pleasant, sandy cove of **Agia Anna** are relatively tranquil spots with shaded tavernas. Most popular of the nudist beaches here are **Paradise**, a long, gradual arc of grainy tan sand backed by rocks and scrub-covered hills, and its companion in Karkingari Bay, **Super-Paradise**. All apart from Agia Anna are very crowded in high season.

You will need either a boat or four-wheel-drive car to get to the **Elia** beach and its fashionable tavernas, but a taxi can take you to the long curved **Kalafatis** beach at the eastern end of the island. Caïques sail out to the isle of Dragonisi, famous for its seals and caves.

On Mykonos' north shore, **Panormos Bay** is much appreciated by windsurfers, with remote **Agios Sostis** being the best of its beaches, while over to the southwest, Agios Ioanis and Kapari are picturesque.

Ano Mera

Standing proudly aloof of the coastal resorts, this inland village is worth a bus-trip for the tranquil **Tourliani monastery** and its 16th-century openwork steeple. It is one of some 360 churches and chapels dotted around the island.

31

DELOS

This island sanctuary is the site not only of great temples, but also the most complete residential quarter which has survived from ancient Greece. Lying at the hub of the Cyclades, the island was a spiritual focus for the ancient Greeks as well as a highly prosperous grain port and slave market, which, at its peak, handled a 'turnover' of 10,000 slaves a day. Its religious festival became a veritable trade fair and Delos was as cosmopolitan a port as Piraeus.

To honour the birthplace of Apollo, pilgrims from the surrounding islands and the city-states of the mainland built great monuments and brought rich gifts and treasure, while their rulers and warriors consulted its oracle. The island was twice 'purified' on Athenian orders: no births or deaths

Bouncing Baby

Walking around this hot and barren rock, you may find it hard to believe that Delos was chosen as a birthplace by Apollo's mother Leto because she had to find some shade. She and his father, Zeus, always looking for variety to spice up his romantic tangles, had made love disguised as quails, reputedly most lascivious birds. Forbidden by Zeus's ever-jealous mistress Hera to give birth in the sun, Leto laboured on the north side of Mount Kynthos, between a date-palm and olive tree – sadly no longer there. Four days later, baby Apollo felt big and strong enough to take off with bow and arrow for Mount Parnassus and Delphi to hunt down his mother's reptilian enemy, Python.

Apollo became the god best epitomizing the Greek ideal: on the practical side he was identified with archery and herdsmen; he also matched art's image of young, manly beauty, patron of music, philosophy and the highest values of civilization.

were permitted here and all graves had to be exhumed and carried off to neighbouring Rhenia (see p.28). The number of people on Delos is still subject to some control, since the only accommodation here is one hotel of 7 beds.

Queasy stomachs should be prepared for a choppy sea on the 30- to 40-minute ride from Mykonos (longer excursions from Tinos, Naxos and Paros). Take good walking shoes for the hike up Mount Kynthos.

Sanctuary of Apollo

If poor weather does not force a landing further around Cape Kako on the northeast coast at Gourna, the standard three-hour morning visit begins with a landing immediately beside the **Sacred Harbour**, which is now silted up. Follow the pilgrims' path to the left along the paved Sacred Way as far as the shrines dedicated to Apollo. On the north side of the **House of the Naxians** is the base of the stone from which Apollo's colossus was built in the 7th century BC. An inscrip-

Within tantalizing picking distance, the fruit of the great god Dionysus.

tion tells that both statue and base were constructed from a single solid block, with graffiti added by Venetians and 17th-century tourists. The statue proved too big for the Venetians to carry off (in 1422) and some pieces they dropped – pelvis and torso – lie behind the 2nd-century BC **Temple of Artemis** (Apollo's sister). A hand is displayed in the local museum and a foot ended up in London's British Museum. **33**

The majestic beasts of the **Terrace of the Lions**, carved from Naxian marble, have become the most celebrated symbol of the sanctuary. Five of the original nine beasts sit up on haunches, mouths roaring, guarding the **Sacred Lake**. Until it was allowed to dry up in 1926 (because of malarial mosquitoes), the lake was the home of swans and geese, descendants of the shrine's holy birds. Now a lone palm tree has been planted in the middle to symbolize the ancient place of Apollo's birth.

The Museum

On a hot day, the museum's airy pavilion makes a cool and pleasant pause before tackling Mount Kynthos and the rest of the archaeological site. Whilst the best of the Delos sculpture is in Athens' National Archaeological Museum, the seven rooms here house a marvellous sphinx, a lion's body with a woman's head from Paros (6th century BC), Aegean Geometric vases and Mycenaean figurines. Particularly fascinating are objects of everyday life from Delos's days as a commercial port, including an interesting selection of medical instruments, utensils, knives, jewellery, keys, combs, anchors and weights.

Sanctuaries of the Foreign Gods

Along the stone mountain path you pass shrines built by the overseas merchants who used to live around the port. The **Syrian temple** (dating from 128 BC), honouring weather god Adad, giver and destroyer of life, was the scene of violent orgiastic rituals until the time when an Athenian high priest decided it was all too much and toned them down. **Egyptian temples** were dedicated to Serapis, god of healing, Isis, goddess of fertility, and Anubis, the jackal-headed lord of the dead.

*L*ions guard the approach to Delos' Sacred Lake; above, mosaic from the Theatre District.

Mount Kynthos

Beyond traces of a small temple to Hera, the climb is worth the effort for the magnificent views. From a platform halfway up, you can take in the whole sanctuary and ancient port-town, while at the summit itself, (112m/367ft), you gain a magnificent view over the Cyclades that once paid the island ancient allegiance. The mountain was inhabited during the Stone Age and shrines were built for Athena and Zeus during the 3rd century BC. It was from this point that the supreme god watched over the birth of his son Apollo.

Theatre District

Coming back down the mountain, turn left towards the sea to the main residential quarter

of the port, around the ancient theatre. On your right as you enter the town is the **House of the Dolphins**, so called for its mosaic of dolphins ridden by cupids. Across the street, the **House of Masks** (popular with visiting actors) has mosaics of theatrical masks and a splendid Dionysus riding a panther. Best viewed from the top overlooking the stage, the fine marble **theatre** (3rd century BC) held an audience of 5,500 on its 43 rows. Beyond the theatre follow the signs over to the left to the **House of Cleopatra**, an Athenian lady whose headless statue, next to that of her husband, welcomes you into their courtyard with its 2,200-year-old well still in working order.

ANDROS

Quietest and greenest of the Cyclades, the first stop on the Rafina ferry-run to Mykonos is popular with many Athenians. Shipping magnates own luxurious villas along the east coast while others have houses with gardens up in the hills, hidden among pine groves and look-

ing down on vineyards in the valleys. Like nearby Tinos, the island is dotted with Venetian dovecotes. Gourmets appreciate the local omelette, grilled octopus, and crushed-almond dessert known as *amygdalota* (see p.111).

Batsi and the Beaches

The ferry stops on the west coast at Gavrion, but the main resort is just to the south at Batsi, built around a charming harbour with good hotels and pleasant beaches. On the cooler east coast, the best beaches are **Nimborio** and **Korthion**.

Andros Town

Like many island capitals, Andros Town is also known simply as Chora ('town'). Built along the ridge of an east coast promontory, its 19th-century neo-classical houses fringe a marble-paved street, which is joined by a bridge to a ruined Venetian castle out on a rock. The Goulandris shipping magnates have endowed the town with three new art institutions:

a **museum of modern art**, exhibiting home-grown talent; an **art gallery** for temporary exhibitions; and an **Archaeology Museum**, which houses finds from the excavations of the ancient settlement of Zagora at the southern end of the island. These include ceramics, domestic objects and sculpture, notably a statue of Hermes.

TINOS

The charms of this mountainous island lie in its sparkling white villages, medieval dovecotes, windmills and farmers' terraces. When the serenity is disturbed, it is not by holidaymakers, but by thousands of Roman Catholics on pilgrimage. Governed by Venice from 1207 to 1714, Tinos has always been the most Catholic island of the Cyclades.

Around Annunciation Day (March 25) and Assumption (August 15), devout invalids are drawn to the port capital of Tinos by the curative powers attributed to an icon discovered in 1823. Indeed, such is the island's popularity that it would be wise to avoid it if possible during the second and third weeks of August.

Tinos Town

The capital's pretty **harbour** forms an almost complete circle and its waters seem miraculously clean enough to attract some very good fish right up to

To keep a precise check on the progress of your sun tan, hedonists recommend white bikinis.

Land Clearance

Nobody quite knows why there are so many dovecotes on Tinos, though the white doves are certainly not complaining. Scholars suggest the Italians' construction of these crumbling square towers, some decorated with patterned tiles, was indulging a common medieval taste for towers like those in Tuscany's San Gimignano. Less fanciful local peasants come up with the equally convincing argument that the dovecotes were just a useful way of piling up the stones littering the farmland.

The bus stops at the foot of **Exombourgo hill**, from where a 90-minute hike will bring you to the summit (565m/1,853ft) to reveal a ruined Venetian castle and fine view over the Cyclades. Other pretty villages are **Loutra**, **Pirgos** and **Falatados**, where you can see nuns of the Kehrovouni Convent making traditional lacework and embroidery.

the dockside. The island caters much more to its Greek visitors than foreigners, but the pilgrimage trade has created an abundance of hotels and a splendid, bustling bazaar. The restaurants and cafés are unsophisticated and have a charm of their own, but sometimes present the foreign tourist with the problem of menus, which like the street signs are usually all in Greek. In the cobbled back streets, the old iron-balconied houses recall the centuries of Venetian rule.

The target of the Catholic pilgrimage is the vast **Panagia Evangelistria** church, reached by a wide thoroughfare sweeping directly up from the harbour. This impressive church stands behind high walls, in a marble and tile courtyard containing nine cypresses and a lone palm tree. A monumental staircase leads up to its porch, which commands a grand view over the harbour and across the water to Mykonos, Delos and Siros, the administrative capital of the Cyclades.

Greek Orthodox tastes have clearly influenced the modern church's highly ornate interior. The ceiling is hung with more than a hundred silver candelabras, and dominating everything is the **icon of the Virgin Mary**, gold-framed and ablaze with fine jewels. Scores of pilgrims' offerings are carefully placed around it to conjure up its curative powers.

Down the main boulevard from the church, an attractive **Archaeological Museum** exhibits Geometric vases from the 10th century BC, enormous amphorae from the 8th and 7th centuries BC, and a notable ancient sun dial.

Interior

Many of the island's 50 or so villages are accessible only by donkey paths – though buses seem perfectly happy to tackle these routes, and a short excusion can be a hilarious adventure. Take, for instance, the afternoon bus from Tinos to **Komi**. Within minutes you are sweeping up, over and around spectacular mountain ridges, beside carefully cultivated terraced fields. The rough narrow road takes you past dozens of tall stone **dovecotes**, of which the Venetians built over 800.

Beaches

Closest and most popular is the extensive **Agios Fokas**, an easy walk east of Tinos harbour. To get away from the crowd, head north of Komi (rough road and donkey path) to **Kolimbithra**, an attractive, secluded sandy beach with a pleasant restaurant up on the hill behind. Even further away, practically at the end of the bus route is **Ormos Isternion**.

SIFNOS

For long a haven of tranquillity (off the main ferry routes), in recent times this sparsely populated island has attracted increasing attention due to its well planned resorts and beach villages. Sifnos is particularly popular with campers.

In ancient times the island was famous for gold and silver mines, which provided it with **39** the wealth to build the most opulent treasury at Delphi, the national sanctuary of ancient Greece, in 526 BC. Today it is claimed that the conscientious Christian can worship every day of the year in a different place, touring the island's 365 churches and chapels.

Ferries dock at **Kamares**, the main port and a centre for the island's thriving pottery industry. A bus will take you inland around the base of Mount Profitis Ilias to the inland capital of **Apollonia**, where white Cycladic houses sprawl across the slopes of three terraced hills. On the north coast is **Kastro**, a gently decaying medieval village on the site of what was probably the island's ancient capital. There is a little **museum** displaying finds from excavations of Mycenaean and Archaic sites.

Along the southeast coast, **Platis Gialos** and **Faros Bay** are probably the best known of the island's beach resorts. For more peaceful and secluded bathing, **Vathi Bay** is accessible by caïque or an invigorating 60-minute walk.

PAROS

Paros, one of the loveliest islands of the Aegean, also has a reputation for being the friendliest. This and its excellent facilities for water sports have made it remarkably popular with Italians and anyone else in love with *dolce far niente*, sweet idleness.

Parikia

On the quayside of the ferry harbour, signs prohibit nude bathing. Rather more inviting is the delightful village of narrow stone walkways beyond. Its shops, archways, churches and houses are all the requisite dazzling white, with shutters blue and green, and courtyards of sweet jasmine and basil, honeysuckle and lemon trees, and canaries in the vine arbour. A particularly exquisite corner of town is the sleepy little quarter around the hilltop **Kastro**, a 13th-century citadel. Savour the fine view from the church of Agii Konstantinos and Eleni (Saints Constantine and Helen) looking over the bay, with Antiparos and smaller islets close offshore and Sifnos (see p.39) looming on the western horizon.

Parikia's cathedral, **Panagia Ekatontapiliani**, is known as the 'Church of 100 Doors' because of its complex structure. It is said to stand over a 4th-century shrine that was founded by St Helen, the mother of Constantine the Great, on her long quest for the True Cross in Jerusalem. Earthquakes and restoration have brought about many changes, most recently from Venetian Baroque back to a hybrid version of its early Byzantine form. In the outer courtyard, five bells hang from a tall cypress tree, which has served as belfry ever since the original tower tumbled down in an 18th-century earthquake. Inside, to the left of the choir pews, the 6th-century chapel of **Agios Nikolaos** is built on Doric columns taken from an ancient Roman site. An impressive bishop's throne stands in the apse of the central Temple of the Virgin. To the right of the main church, the fine baptistery has a sunken font.

*T*he warmly glowing interior of Parikia's Church of 100 Doors – Panagia Ekatontapiliani.

The nearby **Archaeological Museum** houses an engraved marble slab that forms part of the mysterious Parian Chronicle (*Marmor Parium*) – a larger fragment (found in Smyrna) lies in Oxford's Ashmolean Museum. The whole purported to narrate the history of Greece from Cecrops, first king of Athens, down to 264 BC, with a strange mixture of political, religious and literary events. **41**

Some examples of 5th-century sculpture in Parian marble include a large lion and calf relief, a Victory and a winged medusa with snakes. There is also a Roman mosaic in yellow, mauve and blue depicting the labours of Hercules.

Villages and Beaches

Take a bus over to the fishing port of **Naoussa**, where gaily coloured cottage doors on the quayside compete for attention with yellow and russet nets

and the blue, white and orange boats which cram into the tiny, delightful harbour.

Motor launches will carry bathers across the broad bay to the sandy beaches and carved rocks of **Kolibithres**. Further around the island's north east peninsula, Naoussa boats also ply between the fine beaches of **Langeri**, **Agia Maria** and **Platis Ammos**.

Start out from the village of **Marathi** to explore Paros' ancient marble quarries, which were briefly revived in 1844 to provide marble for Napoleon's tomb in Paris.

The bus for Marathi carries on to the very pretty mountain village of **Lefkes**, clearly singled out by its twin-towered, orange-roofed marble cathedral and greatly reputed for its fine ceramics.

At the top of **Kefalos hill** is a gleaming white monastery with marvellous views around the island. Down on the east coast, the pleasant beach of **Piso Livadi** is especially popular with windsurfers. Further to the south, long sandy beaches stretch either side of Drios.

Snorkelling is good almost everywhere, but the best is at **Antiparos** (a 30-minute boat trip from Parikia or 5-minute ferry crossing from Pounda, a small resort south of Parikia). The main island's little sister is also noted for its vast **cave** with stalactites, half an hour on foot (slightly faster by donkey or bus) up the slope of Mount Agios Ilias. In addition Antiparos is a good place for children, with safe, shallow waters (the best beaches are Psaraliki and Soros), as well as camping (the campsite is very well organized). Don't miss the sunsets over Sifneiko Bay in Antiparos Town.

NAXOS

The largest of the Cyclades has much of what you need for the sweet life: groves of orange and lemon trees, figs and pomegranates, excellent honey, tangy cheeses, and a wine that made it a centre of ancient Dionysian revelry. The island also boasts the highest peak in the Cyclades, Mount Zas, at 1,004m (3,293ft).

*A*t Naoussa (left), salted fish dries in the sun; while the boats wait to go out for the next catch.

If Naxians are a little cooler in manner than their neighbours on Paros, could it derive from a natural pride in their august history? The island was well known for its exquisite white marble, with which it became something of a leader in early monumental sculpture and Ionic architecture. It was the dominant power among the islands of the Aegean until its destruction by the Persians in 490 BC, and then it returned to prominence several centuries **43** later as the island-capital of the medieval Venetian Duchy of the Archipelago.

Naxos Town

Looming over the harbour is the town's landmark, the giant **gateway** to the 6th-century-BC Temple of Apollo which was

*T*he gateway (right) is all that is left of Apollo's temple at Naxos, but the olive groves are eternal.

destroyed by the Persians. It stands 5.5m (18ft) tall among white marble ruins on an islet linked by a causeway.

Ignore the port's dull modern construction and head up to the old **citadel**. You climb easily through an enchanting warren of whitewashed cobbled lanes, arches and cheerful tunnels, with boutiques sandwiched between butchers, vegetable shops, bakers and bars. Within the citadel, coats of arms above the doorways bear witness to the island's glorious Venetian past. The church of **Panagia Theoskepastos** has a fine 14th-century icon of the Crucifixion, and the **Catholic Cathedral** contains an even older icon – a rare full-length portrait of the Virgin Mary and Child from the 10th century.

Nikos Kazantzakis, author of *Zorba the Greek* and *The Last Temptation of Christ*, was a pupil in the school that is now the local **Archaeological Museum**. Among its prize exhibits are early Cycladic figurines, and bowls and pitchers excavated from 4,500-year-old tombs found nearby. Look out also for the Mycenaean vases and jewellery, as well as Geometric and Archaic pottery of the 8th and 7th centuries BC.

Just north of town, on **Aplomata Hill**, site of the ancient cliff-edge tombs and a memorial to a World War II resistance hero, you can share with the goats a magnificent view of Paros, Delos and Mykonos.

Excursions and Beaches

The **Tragea Valley**, a haven of peace in the middle of the island, is the best of the inland excursions. Stop off at **Chalki**, with its Italian tower houses. In front of the 17th-century Grazia palace, the Protothronis church has some notable wall paintings. From here, stroll out into a serene countryside of olive groves, lemon trees and cypresses and, nestling among them, Byzantine chapels. You might also visit the charming village of Apirathos, with its Neolithic Museum.

The road through the mountains to the north leads to the coast and the remote little fishing village of **Apollon**. Up on the hill a colossal statue of Apollo lies where its sculptors left it some 2,600 years ago, unfinished because faults in the marble cracked it open.

Many of Naxos' best beaches are south of town. Closest to the capital is **Agios Georgios**, but this can be crowded and the waters are murky. You will find the best sand and most solitude slightly further out at **Agios Prokopios**, the tiny port of **Agia Anna** and **Ormos Plakas**, and coves around the **Mikri Vigla** promontory. On windy days, head over to the north coast where the beautiful and eminently practical marble pebbles of **Lionas** beach will not blow in your face. **45**

AMORGOS

This narrow island, just 18km (11 miles) long, attracts seekers of the quiet life, but is also popular as an excursion from Naxos. On the way, sailing around the south coast, you'll see some of the most spectacular cliffs in the Aegean.

The island's pretty capital, **Amorgos**, with its white houses nestling against a Venetian fort, is a 45-minute drive inland. Northeast from here, on a cliff proudly overlooking the sea, is the fine **Chozoviotissa monastery**, which contains a celebrated icon from Cyprus.

The most accessible beaches are on the northwest coast – **Ormos Egiali** and **Katapola**. Others such as **Kalotaritissa** and **Pharos** can be reached on foot or by caïque.

SANTORINI

Volcanic eruptions and earthquakes have made this island one of the most spectacular in the Aegean. The largest of all these explosions, in 1500 BC, took a bite out of the originally bun-shaped island and turned it into the croissant you see today. The bay is the volcano's collapsed crater, an enormous caldera 11km (7 miles) long.

Sailing into the caldera is a memorable experience. Sheer cliffs exposing starkly-etched volcanic layers rise more than 300m (1,000ft). Two formidable black islets jut out in the middle of the bay, forced to the surface by modern eruptions, most recently in 1950 (another earthquake devastated the west coast in 1956). The almost deserted Thirasia – part of the original 'bun' – now blocks off most of the western horizon as you reach the port of Fira. The gleaming white buildings of the island's capital are strung out along the top of the dark cliffs like an ivory crown.

It's interesting to note that the government, Olympic Airways and some, though not all the ferry operators are gradually reverting to the island's ancient name of Thera, after a Spartan colonizer of the 8th century BC. Thera is the name, too, of the ancient excavated capital in the south, while Fira or Thira is the modern capital on the west coast. The name Santorini is an Italianization of the Byzantine 'Saint Irene'.

Fira and Ia

From the tiny landing stage it is 587 stone-ramped zig-zagging steps to the top (on foot or by donkey), but only a 2-minute ride by cable-car. (You might like to take the donkey back down to the boat excursions around the bay.)

Fira has been well reconstructed since the 1956 earthquake and the many boutiques, especially the jewellery shops, are much appreciated by visiting cruise passengers. A small **museum** has early Cycladic figurines, some Geometric and Archaic pottery and statuettes

Like the icing on a chocolate cake, the town of Fira awaits visitors from passing cruise ships.

from the site of Ancient Thera (see opposite). There are finds from the local Akrotiri excavations, kept here prior to completion of a museum at the site.

Further up the coast, above a tiny fishing harbour, the cliff-top village of **Ia** has done an exquisite work of rebuilding. Highly regarded for its hand-woven fabrics, it is generally a much quieter place to try to find private rooms, or at least to come for a café-terrace view of the grandiose sunset.

Interior

Much of the island is covered with layers of pumice (a light, porous, acid rock) and lava more than 40m (140ft) deep, but under a sun that, even for the Cyclades, is exceptionally dazzling, the plain that slopes east away from the cliffs is unexpectedly green. The volcanic soil supports good crops of tomatoes and grapes, which are used to make a very heady wine. The grape leaves go into the production of sweets and *tsikoudia* liqueur. Quiet inland villages like **Pirgos** make a

pleasant change from the main tourist haunts. Up on a hill, its cobbled streets, white houses and green-doored chapels surround an old Venetian fortress.

The best vantage point overlooking the whole island and south to Crete is the summit of **Profitis Ilias**, 566m (1,856ft). Sidestep the towering radio and TV antennae and visit the **monastery**, which has a notable 15th-century icon of the prophet Elijah (Ilias) (to the right of the main church altar). A **museum** displays icons, illuminated manuscripts and a variety of illustrations of monastic life. If you have a taste for such things, you can see the **ossuary** of monks' bones.

Akrotiri

Excavation at the southwest end of the island is gradually revealing a remarkably intact city founded by settlers from Minoan Crete. Go by bus, bicycle, motor scooter or organized tour for a rare view of a momentous dig in progress.

The site is protected today under the archaeologists' vast

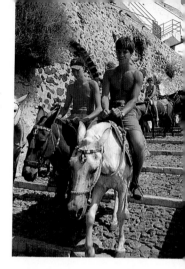

The best way to tackle Santorini's up- and downhill sightseeing is on the back of a donkey.

corrugated iron roof, but for 3,400 years it lay under a crust of volcanic lava. Buried by the 1500 BC eruption and later ravaged by earthquakes, the city didn't emerge again until the 19th century, when it was unearthed during the mining of pumice as construction material for the Suez Canal. Proper excavations commenced only in 1967, revealing a civilization as flourishing and accomplished as that at Knossos in Crete. The works of art uncovered include the great frescoes presently in Athens' National Archaeological Museum, due to be returned to the island.

As you take the signposted tour of the site, its major appeal is the vivid view it gives of the town as a place to live, from houses built of massive hewn ashlar stone, many with walls still standing up to the third storey, to fireplaces, door frames, fine stone stairways, and drainage pipes. Greek archaeologists wryly admit that the system of winter heating is better than that found in most Greek houses today. Among the artefacts left in place are some massive grain millstones and, in the pantry of the tall House of the Ladies, huge decorated storage vessels.

Ancient Thera

Without the benefit of a protective layer of volcanic lava, this ancient hilltop capital is less easily discernible than the **49**

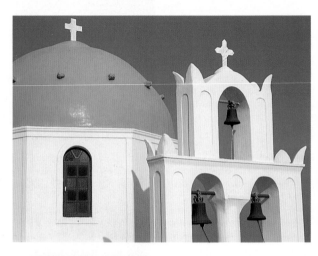

older Akrotiri, but the site remains evocative and certainly worth a visit (approach via Kamari beach). Local guides are on hand to show you around.

Nevertheless, make sure you check the closing times before setting out on a tour.

Although some of the tombs are 600 years older, the ruins date mostly from the 3rd century BC, when this was a garrison town for the Ptolemies, Macedonian rulers of Egypt. Past the Byzantine chapel of Agios Stefanos is the **Artemidorus Shrine**, erected in honour of the Ptolemaic admiral. (After the example of Alexander, many Macedonian leaders raised themselves to quasi-divine status.) As you tour the houses, guides like to point out

The volcanic island of Santorini gets its colour from blue church roofs and brilliant bougainvillea.

the sculpted relief of a phallus with the inscription: 'For my friends'. Make your way up to the **Festival Terrace**, a dance floor for the rites of Apollo, from where there's a view over the southern tip of the island to Akrotiri. At the far south end of the site is the gymnasium.

Beaches

After the initial visual shock, you quickly grow accustomed to the black volcanic sand and pebbles of Santorini's beaches on the east coast. The pebbles, when polished, make particularly handsome substitutes for worry beads. Appreciated for its snorkelling, **Kamari** has a pebble beach at the foot of rocky cliffs but is always busy. **Perissa** has the best sand and **Monolithos**, least frequently served by bus, is by the same token blessedly less crowded.

IOS

This island, called Nios by the residents, is strictly for kids ... kids, that is, from 18 to 30, who enjoy the 24-hour hum (or blast!) of disco music on the beach, in the boutiques and the bars and the cafés. Even when Ios was a hippy paradise in the 1960s, technology barely reached the present decibel level. On a clear day, you can hear Ios from Santorini.

After testing their eardrums to capacity in the bright white capital of **Ios Town**, people sleep it all off in rented rooms and tents around the west coast harbour of **Ormos Iou** and Gialos beach. The popular sandy beach of **Milopotamos** is a 30-minute walk down the coast and there are beaches, accessible by boat, on **Manganari Bay** in the south. Couples like to head east to the secluded beach of **Agios Theodotis**.

Ios is not known for culture, but an 18th-century Dutch digger once claimed to have uncovered Homer's grave here. The grave turned out to be prehistoric, but was not Homer's. **51**

The Dodecanese

The Dodecanese archipelago takes its name from the Greek *dodeka nisi*, meaning 'twelve islands'. This group includes some of Greece's most popular holiday spots, which year in, year out attract thousands of

With a dozen to choose from, island hopping around the Dodecanese is a major pastime.

sun-seekers from around the globe. The island of Kos, verdant and pleasant out of season, guarantees fun in season for those who like their holidays loud and boisterous. The quieter islands include rugged Patmos, something of an aristocrat, with handsome coastal villas and houses around the hallowed monastery of St John the Divine; Kalymnos, proud home of the sponge divers and a Mecca for underwater fishing; Astypalaea, more remote

and sedate, but still cultivating a rough chic; and Karpathos, where the villagers continue to wear traditional costume.

The Dodecanese were united in 1908 against discriminatory Turkish legislation, and were subsequently joined by Rhodes and Kos. The islands came under Italian rule at the time of the Italo-Turkish war in 1912, and were briefly occupied by the Germans before officially being handed back to Greece in 1947. Discernible traces of most periods of history can be found here, as well as glorious beaches and lively nightlife. It is hardly suprising that in recent years the revival of the archipelago's flagging economy has been almost exclusively thanks to the development of tourism.

PATMOS

The little island where St John the Divine had his Apocalyptic vision of the struggle of good against evil is today a haven of serenity. Among the sheltered bays on its rugged coastline, the elegant clifftop villas and the Chora's immaculate white houses nestling up against the

---

Dodecanese Highlights

Patmos: Monastery of St John and Convent of the Apocalypse both celebrate writer of Book of Revelation. *Beaches*: Psili Amos contends for best sand in Aegean; Grigos Bay also has caves. Watersports are best at Meli and Lampis.

Kalymnos: swimmers' island has excellent beach for families at Kantouni, leaving Mirties and Massouri to singles, who may also go nude on nearby isle of Telendos.

Kos: alternative attractions to sun and sand include Knights' Castle in Kos Town and, just outside, ancient site of Asclepium. *Beaches*: all bustling family affairs, with best sand at Tigaki and Kefalos, as well as black sand at Agios Fokas.

fortified monastery, good has triumphed, with a smile. Despite tourism, life remains disarmingly peaceful. Nearly all fruit and vegetables have to be imported and the water tastes rather brackish (bottled water is available). It's a simple life with an appeal all of its own.

Skala and Chora

Sheltered from the open sea on an isthmus in the middle of the island, the harbour of Skala is also the easygoing commercial centre which serves the island capital up on the mountain. Hotels, cafés and restaurants line the quayside.

A road winds up the mountainside past the **Convent of the Apocalypse**. Here, below the Theological College and three chapels dating from the 17th and 18th centuries, is the **Cave of St Anne**, where John is said to have had his revelation. A stone ledge is pointed out as his desk. Three windmills line the route into Patmos Town, with pristine white houses 300 and 400 years old.

Crowning the mountain, the **Monastery of St John** has all the foreboding towers, battlements and ramparts necessary to have protected such treasures as it contained from pirates. Founded in 1098 by the powerful Abbot Christodoulos from Asia Minor, the monastery amassed its riches from

This monk at the Monastery of St John looks as if he goes back to the exalted mystic himself.

'The Time Is At Hand'

Patmos is not much easier to reach now than when the Romans chose it as a penal colony in which political prisoners were sentenced to hard labour. Among them, in 95 AD, was John the Divine (ie Theologian), a Christian activist in Asia Minor. He was condemned, as he wrote, 'for the word of God and for the testimony of Jesus Christ' and opposition to Rome's enforcement of emperor-worship. Between shifts of quarrying stone on the mountainside, John had his mystic visions of the Apocalypse, 'a great voice as of a trumpet' foretelling Christianity's terrible trials and ultimate triumph. His powerful, enigmatic poetry composed in a Patmos cave became the last book of the New Testament, the book of Revelation.

commercial shipping (not to mention a little rake-off from piracy, too). A stairway winds up to the pebble-paved central courtyard, with the monastery church off to the left, built over a temple to Artemis. To start construction off on the proper footing, Christodoulos, whose marble sarcophagus is in the **Founder's Chapel** to the right of the church entrance, destroyed the pagan goddess's statue. North of the nave, over the door to the outer treasury, is an icon of the Apocalypse (1625). Opposite is the 12th-century **Chapel of the Virgin** with an exquisite wooden icon screen (1607). On the east wall are some profoundly solemn icons that were painted around 1190 and constitute fine examples of the unadorned early Byzantine style. Note the superb Virgin with Christ on her lap, flanked by the archangels Michael and Gabriel. Above them is Abraham serving three holy guests, symbolic of the Holy Trinity.

Behind the chapel and left across the inner courtyard, the 11th-century refectory houses long marble-faced stone tables with hollows for the monks' **55** cutlery and pewter. The 13th-century frescoes are in livelier, more emotional style than the chapel paintings. Just beyond, the kitchen has some splendid high-domed ovens. You can climb up to the roof terrace for the wonderful view of Samos to the north and sometimes as far west as Mykonos.

In what is one of the wealthiest monasteries in Greece, the **library** has a very impressive collection of illuminated early Christian and Byzantine manuscripts. Among the most precious are a 6th-century codex of St Mark's gospel, with silver letters on purple parchment and the titles and sacred names in gold, and an 8th-century Book of Job. In the equally fine **treasury** are 200 icons

From Seabed to Bathtub

Each spring, continuing a 3,000-year-old tradition, some 200 Kalymnotes sail around the Mediterranean in search of that luxurious marine animal, the sponge. The departure from Pothia harbour for five or six months is blessed by an impressive quayside religious ceremony, and the return of the fleet, decks laden with sponges, is received with festivities. There is a real sense of relief that the men have survived the risk of death and injury, mostly due to 'the bends', the muscular and respiratory decompression sickness contracted at great depths. Shallow-water sponges have been over-fished, but among the deep-sea varieties, the most desirable is Venus's flower basket.

dating from the 11th century to the modern day, 300 pieces of silverwork, several bejewelled bishop's staffs and a marvellous array of richly embroidered liturgical vestments.

The Beaches

The best sandy beach on the island – and some say in the whole Aegean – is on the east coast at **Psili Amos**. Unless you are sailing, you must bike or hike to get there. A rather more easily accessible resort is **Grigos Bay**, which has some ancient cave dwellings. **Meli** and **Lampis** are both good for windsurfing and water-skiing.

KALYMNOS

Diving and underwater fishing are appropriately major attractions on an island that continues its ancient profession of sponge diving. Whilst largely arid and mountainous in the interior, the island has a dramatic coastline of coves and cliffs, as well as a number of popular caves (Epta Parthenes, Skalies, and Kefalos).

Set against a dark mountain backdrop, the harbour town of **Pothia** stands out as a vibrant splash of colour between land and sea, with its white, green, blue and yellow houses, and shutters framed by flowering rhododendrons. During the ultimate years of Italian occupation, when the Fascists tried to suppress the Greek language and Orthodox worship, Kalymnotes turned their house-painting into a defiant political statement by restricting their colours to patriotic blue and white. A green mermaid sits on the breakwater to comfort the departing sponge divers.

Further up the east coast away from the bustle of the island's capital, the lovely inlet of **Vathi** protects in its transparent blue waters the ghostly remains of an Italian warship sunk by British aircraft during World War II. The valley behind the tiny port is something of a fertile oasis in an otherwise barren interior and makes delightful picnic country. The volcanic soil nurtures groves of mandarins, olives, oranges, and figs, as well as vineyards. **57**

Among the ancient remains on the hillsides are a rock throne at **Rhina** and sturdy walls of hewn stone at **Platanos**.

The best accessible **beaches** are on the west coast of the island. **Kantouni** is a particularly good family beach, while the narrow beaches of **Mirties** and **Massouri** are more popular with the singles crowd. A quick ferry-ride takes you out to swimming, snorkelling and nudist beaches on **Telendos**.

When a great earthquake severed this islet from Kalymnos in AD 535, it submerged an ancient town, still visible under the water.

KOS

Kos is extremely popular with package tourists, who throng its beaches and cafes for several months each year. The island is not to everyone's taste, and depending on your point

---

Doctor Hippocrates

Local tradition claims that the physician of Kos was a centenarian, living from 460 to 357 BC. All we know for sure is that he was a contemporary of Socrates, that he was short in stature, travelled a lot and died at Larissa on the Greek mainland.

In his medical teaching, he broke away from old magic towards more modern therapy based on empirical reasoning. He examined effects of climate and environment on man's psyche and physiology, rejecting, for example, the 'divine' explanation of epilepsy, known as the sacred disease. His treatise on the dislocation of bones was still in use in the 19th century.

The famous Hippocratic Oath began: 'I swear by Apollo the Physician and Asclepius (god of healing) to respect my teacher as I do my parents … not to give poison, though I be asked, nor procure abortion, to abstain from seducing male or female patients and to observe professional secrecy.'

of view you're likely to find it either a Mecca or Hades. It is not without its general appeal, however, for the land is greener than on most of the Dodecanese, its fishermen boast the best catch in the Aegean, and the locally produced wines – *Glafkos* white and *Apelles* red – are particularly fine. Add to that delicious table grapes and internationally renowned lettuce, and it's easy to see why so many people come here for a good time. What's more, the local hot springs are strong in iron for all that ails you and come highly recommended by the island's ancient physician, Hippocrates. So, how to beat the crowds ...? The answer is simple: rent a bicycle and ride a little further.

The optimistically-named 'Hippocrates Tree', planted 2,000 years after the great doctor's life.

Kos Town

The port and Italian-style capital are pleasantly shaded by trees, making exploring during the heat of the day more bearable than it is elsewhere. Overlooking Mandraki harbour, the 15th-century **Knights' Castle**, built with masonry from the Asclepium (see p.60), boasts grounds littered with the jetsam of the island's ancient and medieval history – marble statuary, vases and rusty cannons.

Near a Turkish mosque of the 18th century is an enormous plane tree propped up on crutches and badly in need of a tree doctor. It is old, but not old enough to justify claims that Hippocrates taught in its shade 2,500 years ago. Life and death meet at the fountain **59** beside, which has an ancient sarcophagus for its basin. Hippocrates is also featured – as a subject of both sculpture and mosaic – within the little town **museum** on the main square.

Between Mandraki harbour and the ancient acropolis, the **Turkish quarter** is a colourful reminder that half the town's population of approximately 10,000 is Moslem.

*K*os Town's 15th-century castle provides a dramatic backdrop for the morning swim.

Excursions

Asclepium, a terraced sanctuary and medical school founded in the 4th century BC after Hippocrates' death, lies 4km (2.5 miles) out of town at the end of an avenue of cypress trees. At the lower level are remains of a Roman Bath (1st century AD) which capitalized on the island's sulphur- and iron-rich waters. You will see some fine Ionian column capitals on the middle terrace, but the principal Doric temple of Asclepius is on the upper terrace, from where you have a view of the Turkish mainland, with the Knidos peninsula to the south and Bodrum (ancient Halicarnassus) to the north.

Further west, on the slopes of Mount Dikeos, **Asfendiou** is a commune of white stone houses where, in a courtyard dotted with fig trees, bread is still baked in stone ovens.

Beaches

The most popular beaches are along the north coast at **Tigaki** and beside the fishing village of **Mastichari**. The distinctive feature of **Agios Fokas** on the southeast coast is the unusual black sand, while at the west end of the island, Club Med has planted its flags on **Agios Stefanos Bay**. Not far away, **Kefalos** has some good sandy beaches, lively tavernas and a working flour windmill.

ASTYPALAEA

Still hard to get to and unprospected by tour operators, this island is beloved of the French, which might explain its certain romantic (and some would say snobbish) cachet. Many of the sharply indented coves at the foot of tall cliffs are accessible only by boat and remain blessedly tranquil and anonymous. The handsomely restored white houses of the island's one town spill down the hillside from **Kastello**, with its 13th-century Venetian citadel, beside a row of windmills to the little harbour of **Perigialo**. Down the coast, the charming seaside hamlet of **Livadia** has a nudist beach and the French clientele keeps up the quality of the tavernas. At the northern tip of the island, you can explore the caves of **Vathi**.

KARPATHOS

The population of the island of Karpathos is concentrated in the fertile southern end around **Pigadia**, a modern capital set in the midst of orchards and vegetable fields. Nearby **Kyra Panagia Bay** has a monastery and pleasant beach.

The real charm of the island is to be found in the more isolated north, a broad elongated promontory practically cut off from the south by two large 1,000m (3,300ft) mountains. Boats will take you along the dramatic coastline, with cliffs topped by stunted pine trees, to the little port of **Diafani**. From there, continue by donkey past dozens of windmills on the slopes of Mount Profitis Ilias to **Olimbos**, the oldest and most enchanting village on the island. Maintaining old customs and local folk crafts, the women dress in traditional costume, pleasing themselves rather than the tourists.

61

East Aegean

The three principal islands of the archipelago each produced leading figures in the cultural life of Greece – poets Homer in Chios and Sappho in Lesvos and mystic mathematician Pythagoras in Samos. The proximity of the region to the coast of Asia Minor also made it a constant target for Greece's invaders – Phoenicians, Persians and Turks – motivating Chios, Samos and Lesvos all to play prominent roles in the extended struggle for Greek national independence. In today's more peaceful times, however, visitors can easily take day trips or longer excursions across to the Turkish mainland (see *Island-Hopping* on p.125).

LESVOS

Greece's third largest island (after Crete and Evia) is bustling and prosperous. Covering 1,632sq km (630sq miles), it offers lazy days on pebble or sand beaches, and delightful rambles through pine-forested hills and olive-grove valleys.

Once home to Sappho – not to mention fellow poets Arion and Alcaeus, and the father of Greek music, Terpander – the island has an enduring cultural tradition. Pilgrims come from

---

East Aegean Highlights

Lesvos: fine Archaeological Museum at Mytilini; inland petrified forest between Sigri and Eressos. *Beaches*: best at Mithymna and poet Sappho's home, Skala Eressos.

Chios: three good museums in Chios Town – Argenti Folklore, costumes and porcelain; Byzantine, religious art; and Archaeological Museum, ceramics and terracotta. *Beaches*: all pebble, Nagos and Giossonas on north coast, Emborio to south.

Samos: ancient remains of Heraion sanctuary, complemented by interesting museum in Samos Town.

all over the world to visit the island that inspired Sappho's exalted verse about the young women she loved. More down-to-earth, at Petra on the north coast the Greek government's Secretariat for Sexual Equality has set up a thriving women's agricultural cooperative.

O*n Chios, even after they have picked them, they keep the vegetables freshly watered.*

The island takes an alternative name from its capital of **Mytilini**. This upmarket modern port has a lively, bazaar-like shopping street behind the harbour, with an obligatory but unflattering statue of Sappho. For a good overall view, head up to the **Kastro**, the Genoese-Turkish citadel. At the excellent **Archaeological Museum**, see the villa mosaics (AD 3rd century) which portray Athenian playwright Menander and scenes from his comedies.

Inland from the capital, on the slopes of pine-clad Mount Olympos, lies the lovely hill town of **Agiasos**, reputed for its ceramics and woven fabrics. Up on the north coast of the island, **Mithymna** (also known as Molyvos) is an increasingly popular fishing port with a maze of tall tower houses climbing steeply from the harbour to the Genoese castle. It has a great beach.

On the west side, between Sigri and Eressos, is a fascinating **petrified forest** of conifers and redwoods buried by volcanic ash and later solidified by rainwater and underground springs. Sappho is believed to have lived at the port of **Skala Eressos** (not the more modern inland town). Only fragments of stone wall remain from the days of the great lady, but its sandy beach helps to make the pilgrimage more rewarding.

There are a number of good beaches along the south coast of Lesvos, including **Vatera** and **Plomari**, the latter especially noted for its ouzo.

The Tenth Muse

Plato wrote: 'Some say the Muses are nine, but how carelessly! Look at the tenth, Sappho from Lesvos.' Born in 612 BC, she was forced as a child into exile with her aristocratic family, but later returned from Sicily to marry and bear a daughter, Cleis. At Eressos, she lived in a commune of women devoted to music, poetry and the worship of Apollo. Her odes and elegies treated love with simple tenderness and passion, praising her companions' beauty and goodness in a direct and unaffected manner. Nonetheless, the family is also important in her verse:

Evening, you who bring all,
All that light-giving dawn scattered;
You bring the sheep, you bring the goat,
You bring the child to its mother.

A Selection of Hotels and Restaurants

Recommended Hotels

We list below hotels in three price categories, grouped alphabetically according to the following Aegean island groups: Cyclades, Dodecanese, Eastern Aegean, Northern Aegean and Sporades. Prices will, of course, vary according to season, travel agent's package and unpredictable inflation. For booking directly with the hotel, we have listed phone and, wherever possible, fax numbers (sometimes with Athens area code 01).

Establishments are open all year round unless stated otherwise; 'beachfront' means directly on the beach. As a basic guide to room prices, we have used the following symbols for double occupancy with bath, including breakfast, mid-season (note that in high season, mid-July-September, you are unlikely to find any accommodation under 6,000 drachmas):

▌	below 6,000 drachmas
▌▌	6,000-10,000 drachmas
▌▌▌	above 10,000 drachmas

(International tel/fax code for Greece: 30; for calls from abroad, omit initial 0 on area codes.)

CYCLADES

ANDROS

Andros Holiday ▌▌▌
Gavrion, Andros
Tel. 0282-71384, fax 0282-71097
58 rooms in plush, modern building located on private stretch of headland, roof garden restaurant, lively bar, tennis courts, swimming pool and beach on northwest coast, 150m from town.

Aneroussa Beach ▌▌
Aprovato, Andros
Tel. 0282-41044, fax 01-652-5659
37 rooms, fine beachfront location on west coast, 800m from town. Open May-October.

Myrto ▌▌
Hora, Andros
Tel. 0282-23673
14 rooms and apartments in cosy house in main town, view over harbour, 600m from beach.

Pighi Sariza ▯▯▯
Apikia, Andros
Tel. 0282-23799, fax 0282-23899
42 rooms in country village near hot springs, popular with Athenians, free bus to Andros beaches.

IOS

Aktaeon ▯
Ios
Tel. 0286-91207
12 rooms with seaview balconies on square. Open April-October.

Far Out ▯▯▯
Milopotas, Ios
Tel. 0286-91446
42 rooms, swimming pool, famous for live music at roof garden restaurant. Open April-September.

Manganari ▯▯▯
Manganari, Ios
Tel. 0286-91200, fax 01-363-1904
31 bungalow-style rooms, nightclub, 300m from beach, watersports. Open June-September.

MYKONOS

Ano Mera ▯▯▯
Ano Mera, Mykonos
Tel. 0289-71230
67 rooms in smart establishment, good restaurant, swimming pool, nightclub. Open April-October.

Aphroditi ▯▯▯
Kalafati, Mykonos
Tel. 0289-71367, fax 01-867-4878
135 rooms, bungalow-style with private sandy beach, watersports facilities, swimming pool, tennis courts, nightclub, beachfront taverna. Open April-October.

Carrop Tree ▯▯
Vrissi, Mykonos
Tel. 0289-22038
18 rooms in traditional family-style hotel, good sea view, 800m from beach. Open April-October.

Kouneni ▯▯▯
Tria Pigadia, Mykonos
Tel. 0289-22301
19 large rooms in well-run establishment, 200m from beach. Open April-October.

Ornos Beach ▯▯▯
Ornos, Mykonos
Tel. 0289-22243
24 rooms with seaview balconies, beachfront, watersports facilities, 35km (21 miles) from town. Open April-October.

Petassos Bay ▯▯▯
Platos Gialos, Mykonos
Tel. 0289-23737
21 rooms, bungalow-style, beachfront, pool, 4km (2½ miles) from town. Open April-October.

Philippi   ▥

32 Odos Kalogera, Mykonos
Tel. 0289-22294
13 rooms, flowery garden, open-air restaurant, 500m from beach. Open April-October.

Yannaki   ▥

Ornos, Mykonos
Tel. 0289-23393
39 rooms, restaurant, pool, 200m from beach, 3km (2 miles) from town. Open May-October.

Zannis   ▥

Mykonos town
Tel. 0289-22486
19 rooms, peaceful location near beach, 5 minutes from town. Open April-October.

NAXOS

Anixis   ▯

330 Amfitritis, Naxos
Tel. 0285-22112
18 rooms in pleasant garden, up in old town, sea and mountain view. Open April-September.

Grotta   ▥

Naxos town
Tel. 0285-22215
40 rooms, hillside location amid tavernas and restaurants, friendly family service, temple view, 500m from port. Open April-October.

Kavouras Village   ▥▥▥

Agios Prokopis, Naxos
Tel. 0285-23705
57 bungalow-style rooms, modern, restaurant, swimming pool, 4km (2½ miles) from town 700m from beach. Open May-October.

Mathiassos Village   ▥▥▥

Naxos town
Tel. 0285-22200
110 bungalow-style rooms in gardens, swimming pool, volleyball, tennis courts, 1km (½ mile) from beach. Open April-October.

Nissaki   ▥

Naxos town
Tel. 0285-22876
15 rooms, friendly service in quiet pretty Cycladic house, balconied rooms, tavern on Agios Georgios beach. Open April-October.

Sergis   ▥

Naxos town
Tel. 0285-23195
28 rooms, pool, 10 minutes to town, 5 minutes to Agios Georgios beach. Open April-October.

Panorama   ▯

Amfitritis Kastro, Naxos
Tel. 0285-24405, fax 01-275-8886
16 rooms in dazzling white Cycladic house, located on a hill up above the town, and just 200m

from beach below. Open May-October only.

PAROS

Aegeon   ▥▥▥
Parikia, Paros
Tel. 0284-22153
36 rooms, original design, 300m from beach, 1km (½ mile) from town. Open April-October.

Astir of Paros   ▥▥▥
Kolymbithres, Naoussa, Paros
Tel. 0284-51976, fax 0284-51985
57 deluxe rooms, swimming pool, private beach, watersports, luxury restaurant. Open April-October.

Dina   ▥
Parikia, Paros
Tel. 0284-21325
8 rooms in boarding house, 300m from sea. Open April-October.

Leto   ▥▥
Pisso Livadi, Paros
Tel. 0284-51000
14 rooms, new but quiet charm, 80m from beach, 1km (½ mile) from town. Open May-September.

Narges   ▥▥▥
Aliki, Paros
Tel. 0284-91392
80 balconied rooms, brand new, sophisticated décor, friendly service, swimming pool, 50m from sandy beach, 12km (7 miles) from Parikia. Open April-October.

Parian Village Georgy   ▥▥
Parikia, Paros
Tel. 0284-23186
28 bungalow rooms, view over Livadia Bay, 30m from beach. Open April-October.

SANTORINI (THIRA)

Karlos   ▥▥
Akrotiri, Thira
Tel. 0286-81370, fax 0286-81095
20 rooms in town, modern well-equipped hotel with pleasant service, good restaurant.

Katikies   ▥▥
Ia, Thira
Tel. 0286-71401, fax 0286-71129
7 furnished apartments with terraces and spectacular sea view, roof garden restaurant, 500m from beach. Open April-October.

Mediterranean Beach   ▥▥▥
Vothonas, Thira
Tel. 0286-31167
49 rooms, whitewashed Cycladic-style in beachfront hotel located on east coast, 9km (5½ miles) from Fira town, welcoming family service, swimming pool, watersports. Open April-October.

69

Paradissos ▮▮

Akrotiri, Thira
Tel. 0286-81352
12 rooms, sea view, family atmosphere. Open April-October.

Pelican ▮▮

Fira town, Thira
Tel. 0286-23113
18 rooms in pleasant, traditional town house, centrally located.

Santorini Image ▮▮▮

Messaria, Thira
Tel. 0286-22771, fax 0286-31174
122 rooms and bungalows, huge pool, tennis courts; 6km (4 miles) from Kamari beach, 3km (2 miles) from Fira town.

Stoa Villas ▮▮▮

Ia, Thira
Tel. 0286-71468
6 furnished apartments, traditional-style. Open May-October.

Villa Dolphin ▮▮▮

Megalohori, Thira
Tel. 0286-81663, fax 01-639-9665
6 rooms, beautifully furnished in pretty house. Open April-October.

Villa Elli ▮

Kamari, Thira
Tel. 0286-31266
10 rooms in boarding house, 100m from beach. Open April-October.

SIFNOS

Kamari ▮

Kamares, Sifnos
Tel. 0284-32055
18 rooms in traditional boarding house, 300m from beach.

Platis Gialos ▮▮▮

Platis Gialos, Sifnos
Tel. 0284-31324, fax 0831-22626
22 rooms, roof garden restaurant, watersports, private sandy beach, 5km (3 miles) from town. Open April-September.

TINOS

Aeolos Bay ▮▮

Agali, Tinos
Tel. 0283-23339, fax 01-894-7559
69 rooms with restaurant, swimming pool, 800m from Tinos harbour, boutiques and tavernas.

Leto ▮▮

Paralia, Tinos
Tel. 0283-22791
24 rooms, harbour-front location, interesting roof garden restaurant, 400m from beach.

Porto Tango ▮▮▮

Agios Ioannis, Tinos
Tel. 0283-24411, fax 0283-24416
52 bungalow-style rooms, traditional white Cycladic architecture,

upmarket service, taverna, swimming pool, 200m from beach, 6km (4 miles) from Tinos town.

Tinos Beach   IIII
Kionia, Tinos
Tel. 0283-22626
180 rooms, hotel and bungalow-style, nightclub, pool, tennis, watersports, 25km (15 miles) from town. Open April-October.

DODECANESE (Excluding Rhodes)

KALYMNOS

Kalydna Island   IIII
Kantouni, Kalymnos
Tel. 0243-47880
28 rooms, including bungalows, swimming pool, fine roof garden restaurant, 100m from beach, watersports facilities, 6km (4 miles) from town, but other shops and restaurants nearby.

KOS

Columbia Beach   II
Lambi, Kos
Tel. 0242-28440
58 rooms, swimming pool, watersports facilities, 30m from Faros Beach, 2km (1 mile) from main town. Open April-October.

Hara   I
6 Odos Halkanos, Kos
Tel. 0242-22500
16 rooms in quiet, family establishment, 100m from beach, 500m from town. Open April-October.

Norida Beach   IIII
Kardamena, Kos
Tel. 0242-91231
527 rooms in vast resort complex, nightclub, swimming pool, tennis courts, private sandy beach with watersports. Open April-October.

Pension Alexis   I
9 Irodotou, Kos
Tel. 0242-28798
9 rooms in large house, friendly service. Open April-October.

Ramira Beach   IIII
Psalidi, Kos
Tel. 0242-22891
264 rooms in big resort complex, lush gardens, private sandy beach, nightclub, tennis courts, swimming pool, 4km (2½ miles) from Kos town. Open April-October.

LEROS

Maleas Beach   I
Alcinda, Leros
Tel. 0247-23306
47 rooms, roof garden restaurant, private beach on east coast.

71

PATMOS

Adonis ‖
Skala, Patmos
Tel. 0247-31103
18 balconied rooms with sea view, 700m from harbour.

Artemis ‖
Grikos, Patmos
Tel. 0247-31555, fax 01-804-6678
24 rooms in boarding house, tennis courts. Open May-October.

Delfini ‖
Skala, Patmos
Tel. 0247-32060
12 rooms in welcoming, seafront house. Open April-October.

Irene Liapi ‖
Scala, Patmos
Tel. 0247-31603
Small hospitable boarding house.

Patmos Paradise ‖‖‖
Kambos, Patmos
Tel. 0247-32624
35 rooms, restaurant, swimming pool, 250m from beach on northern peninsula. Open May-October.

Romeo's ‖
Skala, Patmos
Tel. 0247-31070
56 rooms, traditional, 150m from beach. Open April-October.

EASTERN AEGEAN

CHIOS

Chios Chandris ‖‖‖
Prokimea, Chios
Tel. 0271-44401
156 rooms in seafront hotel, roof garden restaurant, swimming pool, 100m from beach.

Golden Sand ‖‖‖
Karfas, Chios
Tel. 0271-32080
108 rooms on beachfront, pool, 4km (2½ miles) from Chios town.

Perivoli ‖
Kambos, Chios
Tel. 0271-31513
9 rooms in very pleasant boarding house with garden taverna.

Poseidonion ‖
Karfas, Chios
Tel. 0271 31927
56 rooms, restaurant, 100m from beach, 4km (2½ miles) from town.

LESVOS

Blue Sea ‖‖‖
91 Plateia Koundourioti
Mytilini, Lesvos
Tel. 0251-23994, fax 0251-23979
61 rooms in particularly modern, efficiently-run and well-equipped

establishment, with nightclub, watersports, 200m from sea.

Delfinia   ▯▯▯
Mithimnia, Lesvos
Tel. 0253-71373, fax 0251-22627
125 rooms and bungalows in resort complex, tennis courts, swimming pool, watersports facilities at private beach on north coast.

SAMOS

Alexandra   ▯
Matamorfosseos 11
Pithagorio, Samos
Tel. 0273-61429
8 rooms, peaceful establishment in large garden. Open April-October.

Chryssopetro   ▯
Pountes Ormos
Marathakambou, Samos
Tel. 0273-37247
12 rooms, hospitable and efficiently-run, good home cooking, 40m from beach on southwest coast. Open June-August.

Dorissa Bay   ▯▯▯
Pithagorio, Samos
Tel. 0273-61360, fax 01 692-8244
310 rooms in very large, modern resort complex, swimming pool, several tennis courts, watersports facilities on private beach. Open April-October.

NORTHERN AEGEAN

LIMNOS

Akti Myrina   ▯▯▯
Mirina, Limnos
Tel. 0254-22681
125 bungalow-style rooms, tennis, pool, private beach, 1km (½ mile) from town. Open May-October.

Kastro Beach   ▯▯
Mirina, Limnos
Tel. 0254-22148, fax 0254-22784
77 rooms, beachfront, 2 minutes from town. Open April-October.

SAMOTHRAKI

Kyma   ▯
Kamariotissa, Samothraki
Tel. 0551-41263
7 rooms with beachfront location.

Niki Beach   ▯▯
Karamiotissa, Samothraki
Tel. 0551-41561
38 rooms close to pleasant pebble beach on outskirts of town.

THASOS

Amfipolis   ▯▯▯
Limin, Thasos
Tel. 0593-23101
47 rooms in pleasant hotel of attractive neo-classical design, with **73**

swimming pool, central location in town with good beach nearby. Open April-October.

Golden Beach

Skala Panagia, Thasos
Tel. 0593-61471
8 rooms in peaceful, secluded location near beautiful beach. Open May-September.

Villa Nikoleta

Limin, Thasos
Tel. 0593-22020
15 rooms set in pleasant garden. Open April-October.

SPORADES

ALONISSOS

Alonissos Beach

Alonissos
Tel. 0424-65281
45 rooms in modern, very well-equipped hotel, with tennis courts, nightclub, swimming pool. Open June-September.

Marpounda

Marpunda, Alonissos
Tel. 0424-65219, fax 01-689-6980
104 bungalow-style rooms in efficient modern complex, nightclub, tennis courts, swimming pool, watersports on private beach. Open April-October.

SKIATHOS

San Remo

5 Fil. Georgiadou, Skiathos
Tel. 0427-22078, fax 0427-21918
31 balconied rooms, attractively furnished. Open April-October.

Skiathos Palace

Koukounaries, Skiathos
Tel. 0427-22242, fax 01-324-5963
223 rooms in luxury modern hotel, roof garden restaurant, nightclub, tennis courts, swimming pool, watersports on Koukounaries Beach.

SKOPELOS

Archontiko

1 Xanthou, Skopelos
Tel. 0424-22049
10 rooms in first-rate traditional boarding house of great charm.

Kyr Sotos

Skopelos
Tel. 0424-22549
12 rooms, old fashioned hospitality in charming traditional boarding house. Open April-October.

Skopelos Village

Skopelos
Tel. 0424-22517
34 bungalow rooms, with swimming pool, 10 minutes' walk from town. Open April-October.

Recommended Restaurants

We appreciated the food and service in the restaurants listed below (alphabetically, and according to the same island categories as for the hotels – see p.66); if you find other places worth recommending, we would be pleased to hear from you. Our choices concentrate on restaurants and tavernas serving local cuisine rather than the less atmospheric 'international' places, pizzerias and other fast-food outlets.

Like hotel rooms, meal prices may vary in and out of season, but by and large they remain within our rating categories:

Ⅰ	under 1800 drachmas
Ⅱ	1800–2500 drachmas
Ⅲ	over 2500 drachmas

Some restaurants close one day a week, some open only for dinner, again with seasonal variations. Some establishments remain defiantly anonymous, identifiable only by the place name itself; eg. *Ornos Beach*. Telephone numbers are given only where a reservation is advisable.

CYCLADES

ANDROS

Dionysos　　　Ⅱ
Messaria
Shady garden taverna located in pretty inland village, piano music, serving dinner only.

Stamatis　　　Ⅰ
Batsi
Situated in centre of village, good variety of traditional Greek dishes efficiently served.

Valmas　　　Ⅰ
Gavrion
Old fashioned taverna specializing in goat meat dishes, light retsina.

IOS

Ios Restaurant　　　Ⅱ
Port
Beachfront, traditional dishes.

Manganari　　　Ⅱ
Port
Near ferry dock, good food, fresh, locally grown vegetables and fruit. **75**

Pithari |
Ios village
Simple fare amiably served in terrace taverna on main square.

Saini |
Ios village
On main street, very popular with locals, but tourists welcomed.

MYKONOS

Dionysos Garden ||
10 Odos Paralou, Mykonos town
Particularly good for tasty, grilled meat dishes.

Elia Beach ||
Paradise Beach
Untraditional taverna, most popular with gay community, but others also very welcome.

Kounelas ||
Mykonos town
Courtyard behind port, family atmosphere, good for seafood, popular with fishermen, dinner only.

Marco Polo ||
Mykonos town
In town centre, very good seafood.

Nikos |
Mykonos town
Old fashioned taverna near town hall, late dining for locals.

Ornos Beach ||
Ornos
Wondeful salads, good traditional dishes in lively taverna on otherwise secluded beach.

Orpheas |
Mykonos town
Robust cooking, near bus station.

Paradise Beach ||
Paradise Beach
Beachfront nightclub atmosphere.

Sesame Kitchen ||
Mykonos town
Bracing fresh salads, vegetarian meals near naval museum.

NAXOS

Janni ||
Agia Ana
Beachfront location, serving good fish, roast chicken, as well as traditional cuisine.

Karnagio |||
Naxos town
Seafront restaurant south of port, fine seafood, but dinner only.

Kastro ||
Plateia Prandunas, Naxos town
Hillside taverna overlooking town and sea, with delicious speciality: locally caught rabbit and onions.

Vasilis ‖

Naxos town
Very lively taverna, friendly service for lusty meat dishes and fresh seafood, dinner only.

PAROS

Apollon ‖‖‖
Parikia, tel. 21875
First class cuisine in very pleasant garden restaurant.

Corfo Leon ‖
Parikia
Good seafood and Greek specialities, situated on seafront square.

Karyas ‖
Naoussa
Well-run seafood taverna beside harbour, good salads, too.

Koutoulas ‖
Parikia
Between the seafront and market, seafood and local specialities.

Lefkes Taverna ‖
Lefkes
Set in typical, old mountain village 14km (8 miles) from Parikia.

Meltemi ‖
Naoussa
Near port, shady seafront taverna serving traditional dishes.

Scouna ‖
Parikia
Pleasant tree-shaded beach restaurant, serving good solid fare, reasonable bargain.

SANTORINI

Akrotiri Cave ‖‖‖
Akrotiri
Beachfront terrace seafood taverna, fishermen's favourite, but serving dinner only.

Amaltheia ‖
Kamari
Taverna serving robust traditional dishes just 100m from beach, but best *after* the swim.

1800 ‖‖‖
Fira town, tel. 71485
Refined dining in elegant décor, located right near volcano crater.

Markos ‖
Perissa
Copious portions served in beachfront family restaurant near cliffs.

Nikolas ‖
Odos Stavru, Fira town
Traditional fare in old taverna.

O Psaras ‖
Akrotiri
Tranquil seafood establishment. **77**

Selena ▮▮▮
Fira town, tel. 22249
Sophisticated cuisine in very quiet location near volcano crater, serving dinner only.

Skaramangos ▮▮
Monolithos
Seafront taverna frequented by locals for island's best seafood – be sure to try the fish soup.

DODECANESE

KALYMNOS

Kambourakis ▮▮
Pothia, Kalymnos town
Tel. 29678
Harbourfront seafood, especially popular with locals, dinner only.

KOS

Angelos ▮▮
13 Odos Psaro, Kos town
Tel. 23979
Robust portions of grilled fish and meat, choose your own cut.

Hippocrates ▮
11 Odos Pindou, Kos town
Robust food in shady courtyard.

Kalli Kardia ▮▮
Mastichari, tel. 51289
78 Grilled fish beside the harbour.

Noufara ▮▮
45 Odos Kamari, Kos town
Tel. 28743
Traditional cuisine, an established favourite with locals.

O Lambros ▮▮▮
14 Odos Salaminos, Kos town
Very good grilled meat and chicken dishes, not far from beach.

Olympiada ▮▮
Kos town, tel. 23031
Solid traditional fare, good service on quiet shady terrace.

Therma ▮▮
Agios Fokas
Simple, no-frills service for fresh seafood beside the water.

PATMOS

Loukas ▮
Skala
Welcoming family atmosphere for solid Greek fare.

Mermaids ▮▮▮
Skala
Conveniently located near ferry-dock, seafood and grilled meats.

Olympia ▮▮
Chora
Traditional cuisine, with splendid view from upper town terrace.

Pantelis |
Chora
Friendly welcome for people with especially robust appetites.

Vagelis |||
Chora
Highly refined cuisine, elegantly served in especially pleasant garden surroundings.

EASTERN AEGEAN

CHIOS

Delfina ||
Chios town
Tasteful cuisine, with friendly harbourfront atmosphere.

Limassi Taverna ||
Limassi port, Mesta
Good fresh seafood served in enjoyable, welcoming ambience beside beachfront.

O Morias ||
Mesta
Rustic Greek cooking served in delightful atmosphere on square in medieval village.

Symposium ||
60 Odos Livanos, Chios town
Good value for money, fairly wide variety of traditional Greek dishes in pleasant ambience.

Theodosiou ||
Chios town
Near the harbour, freshly caught seafood prepared with great attention to personal taste.

LESVOS

Jorgos |
Mytilini
Mainly seafood, south of harbour.

Platanos ||
Plomari
Lively tree-shaded taverna in town centre, extremely popular with locals and visitors alike.

SAMOS

Dionysos ||
Samos town
Pleasant terrace neary ferry-landing, where the wines do honour to the taverna's patron deity.

Plaka |||
Kokkari road
South of Samos town
Highly esteemed and sophisticated cuisine, worth excursion out of town, but serving dinner only.

Samos ||
Plateia Pythagoras, Samos town
Good quality, mainly traditional Greek fare at reasonable prices. **79**

NORTHERN AEGEAN

LIMNOS

Avra ▯
Mirina
Friendly harbourside atmosphere, for grilled meat and fish dishes.

Platanos ▯
Mirina
Delightful atmosphere, tree-shaded terrace ideal for people-watching on main street.

SAMOTHRAKI

Horizon ▯
Paleopoli road
Good quality traditional cuisine in pleasant, peaceful location away from centre of main town.

THASOS

Kalofagos ▯▯
Skala Sotira
Garden taverna much appreciated by more discerning visitors from Greek mainland.

Platanos ▯
Rahoniou
Simple rustic Greek fare on village square, live *bouzouki* music and occasional impromptu dancing, serving dinner only.

SPORADES

ALONISSOS

Naftilos ▯▯
Patitiri
Traditional taverna near harbour, live music at dinner time.

SKIATHOS

Ilias ▯▯▯
Skiathos town
Excellent, highly refined cuisine, but serving dinner only.

To Stelai ▯▯▯
Skiathos town
First-class seafood restaurant.

SKOPELOS

Agnandi ▯▯
Glossa
Beyond harbour, Greek cooking prepared and served with a smile.

Finikas ▯▯
Skopelos town
In upper town, sophisticated meals in pleasant garden, dinners only.

Tsipuradiko ▯▯
Skopelos town
Seafood prepared from distinctive recipes with locally distilled *raki*, very popular with locals.

CHIOS

Proud without being aloof, the striking personality of this island owes much to its Italian past and tormented relations with Turkey, to where day excursions are now offered (to Cesme, 30 minutes by ferry). It lays a claim, beside Turkey's Smyrna and other cities, to be the birthplace of Homer. Its lunar landscapes in the north contrast with citrus groves and almond trees in the south.

Chios Town

The busy port capital tingles with excitement as the evening ferry comes in from Piraeus and local citizens mingle with travellers for the *volta* promenade along the waterfront. The most rewarding of the town's art collections is the splendid **Argenti Folklore Museum** on Platonos Street, with its superb display of old costumes and painted porcelain statuettes of the island's Greek and Turkish peasants. Also worth a visit is the **Byzantine Museum**, set in an old mosque and combining church art with relics of Chios' Venetian and Genoese past. Last but by no means least, the fine **Archaeological Museum** (*Odos Michalou*) exhibits distinctive Chian ceramics and terracotta figures dating from the 7th to 4th centuries BC.

Magic Mastic

The people of southern Chios boast that theirs is the only real mastic region in the world: even a few kilometres north, the 'gum tree' cannot produce the proper resin; while Portuguese claims are dismissed as humbug. So what is special about mastic? Midwives use it as an antiseptic in childbirth; hunters stuff mastic twigs into gutted hares to preserve them; it was an aphrodisiac in the Turkish sultan's harem; and it makes good toothpaste, chewing gum and a 'stinger' of an alcoholic drink.

Just outside town, the beach suburb of **Vrondados** boasts a 'master's stone' where people like to imagine Homer reciting his verse. **Karfas** to the south has a popular sandy beach.

Nea Moni

Make the exhilarating journey west of Chios Town up to this 11th-century monastery hugging the mountainside. A few nuns have replaced the hundreds of monks who once lived here, and they will show you the Byzantine mosaics in the church. See the handsome refectory with its marble table, 18m (60ft) long, and a grim ossuary containing skeletons of Chians massacred by the Turks in 1822. More than any other, this event roused many foreign writers and artists to support Greek independence.

Further into the mountains is the strange, half-abandoned village of **Anavatos**. Byzantine ruins straggle up to a precipice from which women and children jumped to avoid slaughter during the 1822 massacre. The hilltop church is a shell, its frescoes intact. Elderly people occupy a couple of houses, and a few fig trees and pomegranates still bear fruit, but the old bakery's smoke-begrimed oven stands empty.

*D*espite the serenity today of its icons, Nea Moni monastery, right, has known bloody turmoil.

NORTH COAST

The island's many prosperous ship owners live in the pleasant village of **Kardamyla** and like to claim that Homer was

among earlier residents. Their villas look down on the charming port of **Marmaro**. In the same area you will find a couple of good pebble beaches at **Nagos** and **Giossonas**.

South of Chios Town

Beyond Chios airport, in the area of Kambos, old mansions with Italian coats of arms and estate walls enclosing cypress trees, citrus orchards and olive groves stand as a reminder of Chios's Genoese and Venetian masters. Thereafter, you begin to notice the bush-like lentisk trees from which Chians since

antiquity have been tapping a resin of extraordinary powers called *masticha*. Indeed, prior to the War of Independence and the massacre of Chios, the island held a privileged position during the years of the Ottoman Empire because of the mastic trade. Tax relief and better treatment at the hands of the Ottomans were two of the associated benefits.

The centre of the 'mastic country' is the delightful town of **Pyrgi**. Unique grey-white geometric patterns adorn the buildings here, with a subtle touch of colour added by ropes of tomatoes hanging from the **83** balconies. To the west, **Mesta** is an equally charming medieval village where the streets are shaded by arches and tunnels linking the houses from one roof-patio to another. At **Emborio**, 10 minutes' drive south of Pyrgi, is an attractive black-pebble beach. Nearby, there are ongoing (but currently off-limit) excavations of a town that occupied the site from Trojan to classical times.

SAMOS

This fertile island, just 3km (2 miles) from the Turkish mainland, is renowned for its sweet red muscatel wine and a much admired olive oil. Pythagoras, the mystic mathematician, was born here in the 6th century BC but fell foul of the tyrannical ruler Polycrates, and went off to southern Italy to square his hypotenuse. Before him, another great Samian traveller, Colaeus, sailed through the straits of Gibraltar – in those days better known as the Pillars of Hercules – to explore Spain's Atlantic coast. Today, many islanders have chosen to travel right across the ocean and gather in Massachusetts.

The sleepy harbour resort of **Pithagorio** stands on the site of Polycrates' ancient capital of Samos. Northwest of town, bring a torch to explore the **Tunnel of Eupalinos**, which was constructed in the troubled 6th century BC to provide clandestine passage under the city walls. West of Pithagorio, along the coast, are the ruins of the **Heraion sanctuary**, which once boasted the largest temple in the Aegean – 108.6m (354ft) long and 55m (180ft) wide, one and a half times the size of the Parthenon. One column and a few pillar stumps defining the original ground plan are all that survive. The nearby beach resort pays homage with its name Colonna.

The modern capital, **Samos Town**, lies over on the north coast and has a spacious harbour which serves the northern

Over the graceful sweep of Samos Town's harbour, a sprig of oleander.

islands. In the museum, sculptures from the Heraion sanctuary include a massive *kouros* (6th-century-BC temple statue) 5m (16.5ft) tall, and a seated female statue, perhaps of Hera herself. Up on a hill behind the port is the old Turkish capital of Vathi with a charming collection of houses and a fine view across to Turkey. North coast beaches include **Kokari**, **Avlakia** and **Karlovasi**.

On the west side of the island, the highly characterful hill town of **Marathokambos** preserves its leafy tranquillity among impossibly steep narrow streets. From here you can look down on **Ormos**, a little beach resort nearby.

North Aegean

Like the east Aegean, the chief islands to the north remain strongly aware of their Turkish neighbours, with Limnos in particular playing an important strategic role on sea lanes to and from the Dardanelles; but the Balkans are also noticeably close at hand. The climate here is pleasantly cooler, and the landscape greener than in the southern Aegean, and people often come from the mainland to enjoy local gourmet delica-cies, excellent seafood, local wines, and the renowned fruit and nuts of Thasos.

LIMNOS

Facing the Turkish islands of Gökçe and Bozca (Imbros and Tenedos to the Greeks) and the Dardanelles beyond, Limnos is of considerable military importance and its natural shel-tered harbour of **Moudros** is a major naval base. It was from here that the British launched their World War I attack on the Dardanelles, and 900 British Commonwealth soldiers now lie in the cemetery.

Most of the island's charm derives from the leafy capital of **Myrina** on the west coast, where a promontory guarded by a Venetian fortress divides its two harbours, and tradition-al sailors' houses with wooden balconies line the stone-paved streets. The town's well orga-

*L*ike this crochet work, many northern Aegean crafts show the influence of neighbouring Turkey.

North Aegean Highlights

Limnos: good Archaeological Museum in Myrina. *Beaches*: peaceful bathing at both Ziniatha and Thanos.

Samothraki: mysterious Sanctuary of the Great Gods.

Thasos: excellent sculpture in Thasos Town's Archaeological Museum. *Beaches*: Makriamos offers luxury for families and watersports enthusiasts, Krissi Amoudia good for snorkelling.

nized **museum** displays finds from the archaeological sites of Poliochni and Hephaestia. The best **beaches** around the south coast are at **Ziniatha**, **Thanos** and **Plati**, none of which are overcrowded.

SAMOTHRAKI

On Samothraki it is not difficult to believe that the gods of the nether regions live on in the shadows of the rugged granite mountains, fleeing the blinding sunlight just like the island's eternal goats. Of old, Aristophanes, Plato and monarchs ranging from Philip of Macedonia to Emperor Hadrian all came to be initiated into the mysteries of Samothraki's cult of the Underworld. Today,

after a ferry ride from Alexandroupolis to Kamariotissa, you can retrace their steps to the **Sanctuary of the Great Gods** at Palaeopolis.

Ask at the Xenia hotel for admittance to the archaeological site, which is set among a wilderness of rocks and olive trees. Leaving the museum till later, take the path left to the **Anaktoron** (500 BC), an initiation hall with a small adjoining room where novices changed into sacred robes and later obtained their certificate of initiation. The **Arsinoion rotunda** was built in the 3rd century BC by Egyptian Queen Arsinoe. Made of marble from Thasos and combining all three orders – Doric entablature, Ionic cornices and Corinthian columns **87**

– it was the largest circular edifice in ancient Greece, measuring 20m (65ft) in diameter. To the south, sacrificial feasts were held in the courtyard of the **Temenos** (4th century BC). Several Doric columns have been restored to the porch of the **grand Hieron**, where the culminating ritual took place.

On a hill above the theatre, a fountain marks the site of the *Winged Victory of Samothraki* that was taken in 1863 to Paris and now adorns the Louvre.

In the rather more modest **museum** here, be sure not to miss the wonderful Temenos frieze of musicians and dancing girls performing for a wedding of the gods.

Along the north coast, the verdant and luxuriant spa of **Therma** claims to cure infertility (the women's pool is hotter than the men's). It is also the base camp for the exhilarating 5-hour climb up **Mount Fengari**, 1,560m (5,120ft). From what Homer described

Mysteries of the Underworld

The chthonic (netherworldly) Great Gods of Samothraki were of Balkan and Anatolian origin. First among them was Axieros, a universal Great Mother worshipped at sacred rocks. Her subordinate male consort was Kadmilos. Two other gods consigned more specifically to the Underworld, Axiokersos and Axiokersa, were the equivalents of the Greeks' Hades (the deity, not his realm) and his wife Persephone. If the local sages and nobles of antiquity sought initiation into the dark mysteries of this Underworld, it was as a place of moral judgment without the horrific overtones of evil to which Christian ideas of hell have accustomed us. Initiation entailed confession, purification and moral resolutions to lead a better life. Of the Samothraki initiation ritual, we know only that it was performed at night and conducted in the Thracian tongue.

as the 'topmost peak of wooded Samothraki', you, like Poseidon, can look out over the battlegrounds of Troy on the Turkish coast.

THASOS

Famous in ancient times for its fine white marble and heady wines, this most northerly of the Aegean islands still cultivates a taste for the good life. (Wine is now imported from the mainland.) A good ferry service from Kavala takes you to a serene island, green with pines and chestnut trees and a silver filigree of olive trees and beaches. Here you'll find people more friendly and easy going than on the mainland.

The modern port of **Thasos Town** (also known as Limin) is constructed among ruins of the classical city and contains a 5th-century-BC rampart, including towers and gates. The wall rises steeply from the harbour to the ancient **theatre**, a lovely creation with a proscenium dedicated to Dionysus where classical drama is performed in summer. Further up,

a rock-hewn shrine to Pan has a carved relief of the god piping to his goats.

Near the old harbour, the **Archaeological Museum** has some fine sculptures in local marble, most notably a colossal *kouros* (temple statue, 6th century BC) of Apollo carrying a ram, and a handsome head of Dionysus (3rd century BC).

Beaches

Just 2km further southwest, sandy **Makriamos** is a luxury beach resort providing almost every sport under the sun (and a couple in the shade), especially skin-diving, fishing and sailing. **Krissi Amoudia** is the main beach for the snorkelling fraternity and has some good seafood restaurants, too, while Limenaria is generally popular. Head south to **Kinira** for some gentle surfing. In the old quarries down at **Aliki**, the marble still bears the scars of ancient picks. On your travels, taste the honey and Thasian preserves (*glika tou koutaliou*) of green figs or green walnuts, cooked over wood fires. **89**

The Sporades

The Sporades (literally 'scattered' islands), just east of the Pelion peninsula, are an attractive mixture of well organized (sometimes almost too well organized) beach resorts and traditional old fashioned places where the Greeks themslves go to relax. Although there are plenty of fine sand beaches, in this region where the *meltemi* wind can blow quite fiercely you will quickly appreciate the advantage of the smooth pebble beaches here, too.

SKIATHOS

Boasting well over 60 beaches – both fine sand and smooth pebble – and several bays and harbours for yachts and small craft, Skiathos is *the* beach resort island. Dense forest blankets the interior with beech, evergreen oak, chestnut, pine and the low arbutus strawberry tree – its 'strawberries' are enticing, but inedible.

Skiathos Town

Surrounded by wooded hills, the island's capital has plenty of cheerful cafés and souvenir shops. Cross the causeway to **Bourdzi** islet for its good view of the harbour.

Buses run west from Skiathos Town to the **beaches** on the **Kalamaki peninsula**, the most popular of these being **Kanapitsa**. At the west end of the island, the much celebrated

*S*kiathos Town is as popular with vacationers from the Greek mainland as it is with foreigners.

Sporades Highlights

Skiathos: best for *beaches*. Kanapitsa on Kalamaki peninsula most popular, but finest sand at Koukounaries. Quieter are sand dunes of Mandraki and secluded Agia Eleni. Nudists hide out at Banana Beach. For pebbles, head for Lalaria.

Skopelos: black pottery in Chora, icons in Church of Christ. *Beaches*: families enjoy Limnonari, nudists go to Velanio.

Skyros: two good museums in Chora – Faltaitz for folk arts; and Archaeological Museum for Mycenaean ceramics. *Beaches*: most popular is Magazia, with quieter sand and a pebble cove at Pefkos.

Koukounaries beach has fine sand stretching roughly a full kilometre. More secluded on the west coast is **Agia Eleni**, facing Mount Pelion, and not far away is the nudist Banana Beach (Krassa). Further north, amid beautiful pine trees and backed by russet cliffs are the sand dunes of **Mandraki**. The best of the pebble beaches is on the north side of the island at **Lalaria**.

Kastro

To get away from the crowds, head out to this ghost town, which now stands in ruins on its own north coast promontory. Islanders constructed their refuge here in 1538 while the Turkish pirate Khair ed-Din, better known as Barbarossa, was slaughtering the population of neighbouring Skopelos. There are boat tours, but you can also drive northwest of the capital and take a 30-minute walk through the forest out to the coast. The fortified town with only a drawbridge linking it to the rest of the island once had 300 houses. Of its original 20 churches, only two survive. One of them, the **Church of Christ**, still contains icons and a carved wooden altar screen. **91**

SKOPELOS

The islanders here are remarkably amiable, and the women are especially proud of their traditional costume – flowered silk skirt, velvet jacket with billowing sleeves, and a light silk kerchief on the head. The capital, **Skopelos**, is a classical Aegean town of dazzling white houses with blue-slate or grey-stone-tile roofs, crowned by a **Venetian castle** at the top of the hill. The town's craftsmen produce fine black pottery. Visit the 17th-century **Church of Christ** to see the icons and altar screen, and try venturing into the island's green hilly interior, which is dotted with monasteries and chapels.

Beaches

The best beaches are on the south and east coasts, particularly **Limnonari**, which also has good taverns. Nudists undress over at **Velanio**, while the nearby beach at **Stafylos** is named after the Cretan general believed to have colonized the island after the collapse of Mi-

noan civilization. His grave was found here in 1927 along with a gold crown, weapons and burial offerings which are now displayed in Volos museum on the mainland. In the southwest, worth checking out are **Panormos** beach and the pleasant beach and fishing village of **Agnondas**.

ALONNISOS

This simple little island inhabited mainly by herdsmen and fishing folk holds great appeal not only for swimmers and snorkellers, but also for hikers, who enjoy tackling its pine-clad, thyme-scented hills. The limpid waters around the island have been declared a marine conservation park. The best pebble beaches lie scattered around the **Kokkinokastro peninsula**, a 30-minute boat excursion from the main port, **Patitiri**. You'll find that the taverns in the yachting harbour of **Steni Vala** serve the island's finest seafood. Alonnisos also has a very beautiful **chora**, with charming architecture.

SKYROS

Out on its own to the east, the largest of the Sporades islands splits into two distinct halves on either side of an isthmus. In the south, oak, beech and pine forests cloak a range of rugged mountains, while the north is fertile with farmland and cattle pastures. The famous Skyrian miniature ponies, descendants of an ancient breed known as Pikermic, are kept in a hillside pasture by the port of **Linaria**.

The island capital, **Skyros**, is a pretty town of white houses. The **Faltaitz Museum** displays embroidery, basketware, copper and furniture. The fine **Archaeological Museum** has Mycenaean ceramics. A hilltop **fortress**, part Byzantine, part Venetian, occupies the site of the ancient acropolis from which King Lycomedes is believed to have pushed Athenian hero Theseus to his death.

Amid olive trees on Mount Kokhilas is **Rupert Brooke's grave**, where the English poet of World War I died in 1915 at the age of 28, on his way to fight in the Dardanelles. His poem for all English soldiers served as his own epitaph:

If I should die, think only this of me:
That there's some corner of a foreign field
That is for ever England.

To the north is the popular **Magazia beach**. The best of the rest is **Pefkos** in the west.

*S*kyros fishermen are known among the Sporades, their delicacy being the kanias giant crab.

What to Do

One of the chief wonders of ancient Greek civilization is how they found the time and energy to do it all. It was just as hot in those days and there is no evidence that they confined their building, sculpting, thinking and writing to winter time. So we have no excuse. Bear in mind that siestas are even more enjoyable if you do something in between. Without wishing to suggest anything too much like work, here are a few ideas.

Shopping

Walk into the bazaar with your eyes wide open and you will soon sift the wheat from the chaff. Rugs, pottery, furs, gold and silver jewellery, ranging in price from moderate to expensive – these are some of the bargains to look out for.

Antiques. Anything that predates Greek independence in 1821 is considered an antique and must have an export permit if you wish to take it out of the country. Customs officials have a keen eye open for the larger pieces, while less conspicuous items such as coins and terracotta or bronze figurines are highly likely to be fake anyway. Good replicas of Byzantine works and various modern icons in the traditional style are also on offer, with the best bargains in the museumshops and monasteries.

Clothes and Leatherware. The folk look is shown off best by the Greeks themselves. If you are determined to go native, try a fisherman's sweater, a pair of sandals or some hand-made boots. Mediocre workmanship on the mass produced leather luggage, however, does not justify the vast displays it commands at every resort.

Folk Art. The hand-made creations of traditional artisans maintain a high standard and a remarkably low price. The discerning buyer will soon notice that styles in wood-carving, fabrics, lace and embroidery differ considerably from the Cyclades to the North Aegean. Take a look at the folk art museums – notably the Faltaitz on Skyros, and Argenti on Chios – where you can see, unhustled by shopkeepers, the best of regional production. Many of the islands' museums also have good shops with knowledgeable assistants on hand to advise you – though the range of goods may not be as wide as you will find in bazaars and specialist craft shops.

Window shopping for silver on Mykonos, left; these cotton sweaters are cheaper, below.

Jewellery. The best choice is to be found at cruise ports like Mykonos and Santorini. The styling of gold and silver jewellery is often dictated by ancient history rather than local custom. While you'll still find Byzantine-style, silver filigree, designers now reproduce the fine jewellery of Minoan Crete or the Macedonia of Philip and Alexandria. Gold or silver is sold by weight, with a relatively tiny cost for workmanship. **95**

*A*eons of history are evoked by replicas of traditional busts.

Pottery. The ancient art is far from dead. Sifnos, Chios, Skyros and Naxos are all home to some of the best manufacturers in the region. The pottery of the Dodecanese and Rhodes in particular is admired for its vivid versions of Turkish design. The famous Lindos pottery with tulips and roses on a dark green background is now made on Rhodes and sold elsewhere in the Dodecanese. Attractive replicas of Minoan and Geometric-pattern vases from Crete are available on Santorini and other Cycladic islands.

Rugs. The celebrated shaggy *flokati* rugs have not changed much since they first draped the walls and floors of Minoan residences in ancient Thera, or served as winter bedcovers for Ariadne on Naxos. They are priced by the kilo (a square metre weighs about 2.5 kilos). You'll soon be able to tell the difference between machine-made rugs and the much more tightly packed handmade ones. Sheep's wool is spun from fibres into yarn and then looped on a loom to create a rug that is straggly on the surface and matted underneath. The fluffy but compact finish comes from being soaked for a few days under running water. Rug-like *tagari* shoulder bags, popular in the sixties, are now making something of a comeback.

Souvenirs. Trinkets and mementoes are in plentiful supply, usually displayed under a bold sign saying 'Greek Art'. While few match this ancient seal of aesthetic quality, any artistic shortfall is often made up for by their imaginative design. Borrowing ancient monuments, shopkeepers offer an array of kitsch – little white Corinthian columns as bottles of ouzo, the Charioteer of Delphi as a lamp, the Athens Poseidon as a garden dwarf.

To Buy or Not to Buy

The following list will give you some indication of what specialities to look out for on which islands.

Chios	Fruit preserves and red soil pottery.
Kalymnos	Sponges.
Kos	Limited duty-free bargains (as on the other Dodecanese islands) in imported items like porcelain, textiles, glassware and liquor; also sculptures of animals made from *porolithos* (a volcanic rock).
Lesvos	Ouzo.
Limnos	Honey.
Naxos	Antiques, brightly painted gourds, pottery and *kitro*, a liqueur made from leaves of lemon trees.
Paros	Souvenirs made from *lychnitis* (competes with Carrara as the world's finest marble).
Patmos	Duty-free bargains, but some items can be much more expensive than on Kos.
Samos	Wine.
Sifnos	Decorated pottery.
Skyros	Pottery, wood carving, dresses, scarves and *trohathia* (made-to-order sandals with thongs).
Skopelos	Black pottery.
Thasos	Pine, thyme and orange *kirithra* honey.
Tinos	Black and white marble, basket-work, icons, incense and offertory candles.

CALENDAR OF EVENTS

Despite their country's rapid modernization, Greeks still seem strongly attached to old traditions, cultural, religious and pagan.

January 1: New Year's Day or *Protochronia* – St Basil's Day, in whose name you may be offered a sprig of basil, symbol of hospitality. Popular processions on Andros and other islands.

January 6: for Epiphany, a cross is thrown into the harbour and young men dive into the ice cold water to retrieve it. The one who recovers it receives a special blessing and a crucifix.

February/March: Carnival is celebrated with costumed parties and processions on Chios, Lesvos, Paros, Skyros and Karpathos.

March 25: Greek Independence Day, with military parades.

Clean Monday: first day of Orthodox Lent, house cleaning, laundry and kite-flying; frugal meals of *lagana* unleavened bread and *tarama* (salty fish-eggs), olives without oil and *halva* sesame cake.

Orthodox Easter: most important of Greek religious holidays. Candlelit processions follow a flower-bedecked bier on Good Friday. On Holy Saturday at midnight, a priest hands down the sacred flame from candle to candle for each household to light a lamp. On Sunday, lambs are sacrificed for roasting, as in ancient Greece at the approach of spring. Festivities on Karpathos and Santorini.

April 23: St George's Day, horse races, dancing on Limnos, Kos.

May 1: May Day processions and flower festivals.

May: ceremony for sponge-fishermen on Kalymnos.

May/June: bull ceremonies on Lesvos.

August: drama festival on Thasos; *Hippocratia* festival on Kos.

August 15: Assumption, celebrated with processions on Tinos and Lesvos, fish and wine festival on Paros.

October 28: National *Ochi* 'No' Day commemorating Greek defiance of Italian invasion in 1940.

December: carols (*kalanda*) on Christmas Eve and New Year's Eve; sailors' torchlit procession for New Year's Eve on Chios.

Entertainment

If you look around, you'll find there is a great deal more to the islands' nightlife than discos and canned music at the beach barbecue.

Music and Dance

When not sounding from the ubiquitous 1930s vintage radio or record player, music is usually performed on a *bouzouki*. Some purists claim that the long-necked mandolin-like instrument, which has given its name to both the music and the night clubs where it is played, is Turkish rather than Greek.

What you may find yourself doing after dinner, the *syrtaki* dance popularized by Anthony Quinn's Zorba, is in fact a combination, invented for the film, of several distinct traditional dances. Their old Greek origins are testified by the formations of dancers in friezes on Thera's Minoan frescoes or classical Cycladic pottery.

The *zeybekiko*, which originates from Asia Minor, is an introspective dance of medita-tion with the man swaying slowly, his arms outstretched, eyes half closed, leaning backwards, bending his knees, occasionally taking long steps sideways or forwards like a drugged flamingo and making a sudden twist or leap. This blossoms into the *khassapikos* or butcher's dance in which two or three men link arms and join together swaying, dipping and stepping to the signal of a shout or squeeze of the shoulder from the lead dancer carrying a handkerchief. All these dances are linked in turn to the sedate, majestic *tsamiko* performed by the *klephtes* rebel brigands of the mountains, and dragging *syrtos* round-dances typical of the Aegean islands. Greek women often favour the slow *syrtos* dances, performed with demure modesty.

Your best chance of seeing the more traditional dances is at country weddings and festivals. If you join in a more riotous version in some taverna where they take to smashing dishes and tossing gardenias to the ladies, remember that both will be added to your bill. **99**

The alternately harsh and plaintive popular music which inspired the Greek composer Mikis Theodorakis was the *rebetiko*. This was created by the militant urban youth of the tempestuous 1920s after the mass exchange of Turkish and Greek populations. On the islands of Thasos and Samothraki in the north, you may also hear a *gaoda* (bagpipe), *zourna* (oboe) and *floghera* (shepherd's flute).

A delightful trio of dancers on Kos waiting for their Zorba to whisk them away.

Theatre

Even if you do not understand a word, an evening of classical Greek drama can be a magical experience. On Thasos, the ancient tragedies of Aeschylus, Sophocles and Euripides or the comedies of Aristophanes are performed in the open air amphitheatre as part of the island's August drama festival. These plays are performed in modern rather than ancient Greek, which most of today's Greeks would have a hard time following. To get maximum enjoyment from your evening, try to read the text in English or at least a brief synopsis of the plot before you go.

Each island has at least one **cinema** (outdoor or indoor) and foreign films are frequently shown, in the original language with Greek subtitles.

Sports

An ancient Olympic champion returning to see what's going on in Greece these days might be puzzled by all that swimming. In days of old, swimming was something you did to escape a shipwreck, not for sport. Nowadays, on the other hand, not many people will be doing much running, jumping, boxing or wrestling, and the frisbees on the beach mostly fall short of an Olympic discus. Still, imagine how the nymphs would look on jet-skis and what Icarus, the first man to try to fly, would make of paragliding, both popular now.

The seas around the islands are warm enough for swimming from May to mid-October. For sports where you will want to rent equipment, obviously the major resorts are the places to go. In even the tiniest, secluded fishing harbour, however, you should be able to find a little caïque to hire.

Swimming. With hundreds of beaches, choosing the perfect one is sometimes difficult. The ideal beach is not always the one with the finest sand, so locate a few pebble beaches for days when the *meltemi* wind is blowing. Rock ledge beaches have the considerable advantage of being uncrowded, but use plastic sandals if you are going to paddle around on the rocks. Nudist bathing is officially forbidden, but in practice you'll find several beaches where people take it all off. The criterion for this seems to be relatively secluded places not frequented by families or by Greeks themselves. (See our beach listings, p.29.)

Snorkelling and Diving. The joy of underwater swimming around the Greek coasts is not just for the marine fauna and flora you will see, but the occasional vestiges of ancient ports and cities. However, in some places like Psathoura or Pelagonesi off the north coast of Alonnisos, in order to avoid disturbing the archaeological sites and ancient shipwrecks, only snorkelling is permitted. The coasts of Alonnisos are a marine conservation park.

101

Windsurfing and Waterskiing. Equipment can be hired at all the major resorts. There are particularly good schools for waterskiing on the islands of Chios, Lesvos and Skiathos. Adepts of these sports are increasingly being shunted away from popular family beaches. Opportunities for straight surfing are fairly limited – nothing on the Hawaiian scale, though Mykonos' Ormos Bay attracts serious aficionados.

Sailing. Even just chugging around in a caïque fitted with an outboard motor, you can face the open sea and imagine yourself as Jason with or without his Argonauts. If you fancy exploring the Aegean as a full-blown Odysseus, the National Tourist Office (see p.136) can help you charter a yacht at Piraeus. Renting smaller sailing

W aiting for the breeze to turn, board and sail lie expectantly beside a Samos beach.

vessels is possible at any fair sized port. Skiathos offers first class sailing facilities.

Fishing. Fishing from shore or from a boat can bring in seabass, swordfish, dentex and a host of eastern Mediterranean fish that have no equivalent English names. No special licence is needed, but underwater spear fishing is restricted. Enquire at the local tourist office. It is sometimes possible to hitch a ride with friendly professional fishermen who go out at night with flare lanterns. Another useful friend is the local taverna chef who might cook your catch.

Tennis. Many big resort hotels have courts, the best being on Skiathos, Limnos, Santorini, Mykonos, Alonissos, Kos and Patmos. Some are floodlit.

Hiking and Climbing. Despite the mountainous configuration of the Aegean islands, there are no serious peaks to be scaled, but hiking into the interior is a true joy. Tourist offices can help with walking maps. Keen ramblers favour Tinos and Paros in the Cyclades, Patmos and Karpathos in the Dodecanese, and Chios and Lesvos – for its petrified forest – in the east. The region's highest mountain is on Naxos, Mount Zas, at 1,004m (3,293ft). A popular climb is Mount Fengari on Samothraki, from where you can gaze, like the sea god Poseidon, across to the Turkish coast where the Trojan Wars were fought.

Horse Riding. At the spa resort of Thermi on Samothraki, horses can be hired for enjoyable cross-island treks.

Children

With a little forethought, the Greek Islands can be a great place for kids. One of the best ways to get them to do what *you* want is to start or end the day at the beach or swimming pool. When at the beach, make sure that there is plenty of safe shallow bathing available for the children, as lifeguards are rare or non-existent.

103

This modern café on Chios has revived the centuries-old art of sgrafitto wall-decoration.

Here are some other attractions for the whole family:

Karpathos: in the village of Olimbos, even the children go around in traditional costume.

Sifnos: at Vathi, the potters come to the beach to model their wares. This is also a great island for family camping.

Paros: visit offshore Antiparos, and if the children are not old enough for snorkelling or scuba diving, take them on donkeys to see the stalactites and stalagmites in the cave on Mount Agios Ilias.

Chios: kids and adults alike love the collection of porcelain statuettes of Greek and Turkish peasants in Chios Town's Argenti Folklore Museum.

Skyros: famous for its miniature ponies, which are kept in a hillside pasture near Linaria till at least late spring. The Faltaitz Museum in Chorio has a great collection of folklore.

Kos: the Knights' Castle is the stuff of Crusader legend, especially for lovers of *Dungeons and Dragons*.

Samothraki: everybody enjoys the legends of the Trojan Wars, whether in film, comic strip or Homer's *Iliad* epic. Sturdier children can join you on a trek up Mount Fengari for a view of the Turkish coast where the battles were fought.

If you're there at **Carnival** time (February/March), take the kids to see one of the fine processions on Lesvos, Chios or Paros (see the Calendar of Events on p.98 for festivals).

Eating Out

The essential ingredients of a Greek meal have not changed much since Plato's Banquet. Lamb, goat and veal are charcoal grilled just as they were by Agamemnon's soldiers at the gates of Troy. Red mullet and octopus, beans and lentils, the olives, oil and lemon, basil and oregano, figs and almonds, even the resinous taste of the wine all form a gastronomic link between ancient and modern Greece. The honey with your yoghurt was in the nectar of the gods.

After the pleasant fatigue of a day at the beach or a challenging pilgrimage to an old sanctuary, a traditional Greek dinner offers a time of total relaxation. Ambience is more important here than *haute cuisine*. Greek cooking makes no pretence of emulating the sophistication of the French or the infinite variety of the Chinese. Yet the people's natural zest for life can always conjure the many savoury ingredients of a Mediterranean market into

something wholesome, satisfying and not without its own enticing subtlety.

Where to Eat

You will never discover the adventure of Greek cooking if you stick to your hotel dining room. Playing it safe to palates intimidated by anything new, hotel cooking remains unadventurous. Even when a 'local speciality' is offered, like the

*H*ow can anyone resist a Mykonos tavern sporting such a charming sign as this?

yoghurt and cucumber appetizer known as *tzatziki*, the essential garlic is imperceptible, on the assumption that it is likely to upset north European or American guests.

The problem posed by hotel restaurants may also be true of some tavernas situated in the very centre of the tourist traffic. Many find it most profitable to cater to a fairly low common denominator. Therefore, try whenever possible to follow where the Greeks go. In port towns, for instance, the Greeks often keep away from the crowded harbourside establishments. In the backstreet tavernas, among people who will tolerate much but nothing bland, you can enjoy the real zing of garlicky *tzatziki*, often rendered even more refreshing with an added touch of mint.

Look out for three varieties of snack bar. For yoghurt or cheese snacks, try the *galaktopolio* (dairy counter). The *psistaria* (grill) serves different kinds of meat kebab. For a better choice of desserts than is served in restaurants, try the *zacharoplastia* (pastry shop).

You will also come across the traditional Greek *cafeneion* (café), particularly in inland villages. However, this is more of a men's club than a public café, popular for political debate, backgammon and especially strong coffee. Strangers are not refused admission, but

*F*or those who can't understand the Greek on the wall menu, right, the table version is multilingual.

the place is considered, if not off limits, then at least a haven for Greeks among themselves.

When to Eat

If you decide to 'go Greek' and accept wholeheartedly the venerable institution of the afternoon siesta, you may want to modify your meal times. The Greeks themselves get in a prolonged morning's work and have lunch around 2pm, siesta until 5, maybe work a little more until 8.30 and then dine late around 9.30pm. The restaurants will serve you earlier, from midday and early evening, but you will miss the more authentic Greek scene if you just keep 'tourist hours'.

The strenuous effects of the climate and all that sightseeing may also persuade you – contrary to local custom – to stick to a light lunch and save the main meal for the evening.

The Menu

The tantalizing thing about the many tasty Greek specialities is that only a fraction of them

are available at any one time. The menu printed in English frequently lists them all, but only those items with a price against them are being served that day. Rather than submit to this frustration, see if you can do what the Greeks do and go

back to the kitchen to find out what is being cooked. There the cold appetizers are arrayed in glass display-cases. Cuts of meat and the fish-catch of the day are lying ready in glass-windowed refrigerators. Hot dishes are simmering on the **107** stove in casseroles from which the cook will take off the lid for you to peek in and sniff. The management is often more than happy for you to point out your choices here and avoid later misunderstandings.

Remember fish and meat are usually priced by weight, so that the size you choose in the kitchen becomes your responsibility when the bill arrives.

Appetizers

It is the Greek custom to eat appetizers (*mezedes*) with an aperitif of *ouzo* and cold water, separately from the main meal. For convenience, they are usually served at resort tavernas as part of the dinner. Nonetheless, the essence of the *mezes* is its slow enjoyment, something not to be gulped down but savoured for itself.

Besides that yoghurt-and-cucumber *tzatziki*, the range is impressive: *tarama*, a creamy paste of cod's roe mixed with breadcrumbs, egg yolk, lemon juice, salt, pepper and olive oil; *dolmas*, little parcels of vineleaves, stuffed with rice,

and sometimes pine kernels and minced mutton, braised in olive oil and lemon and then served cold; aubergine (eggplant) salad (*melitzano salata*) puréed with onion and garlic; the very common Greek salad (*salata horiatiki*, literally village salad), a refreshing mixture of tomato, cucumber, *feta* goat cheese and black olives; small pieces of fried squid (*kalamarakia tiganita*) or cold marinated octopus (*chtapodi*) made into a salad; cheese pies (*tiropitakia*), small pastry triangles of goat and ewe cheese; marinated mushrooms mixed with white beans; a spicy trio of *pastourma*, thin peppery, garlicky slices of dried mutton, beef or goat; *loukanika*, spicy sausage; *mithia,* mussels; and, of course, dishes of olives, green, black, brown or silvery.

Soups

Resort tavernas often do not like serving soups, because of the temptation to treat these fulsome dishes as a meal on their own. However, the best known is light enough to appear as an accompaniment – *avgolemono*, egg and lemon with chicken broth, thickened with rice. At Easter, join the Orthodox Greeks who break the Lenten fast with the traditional *magiritsa* lamb tripe soup, spiced and cooked with lettuce, egg and lemon. Santorini in particular is of repute for its bean soup (*fassolatha*), while connoisseurs swear by Sifnos-style chick pea soup (*revythia soupa*) with onions, olive and lemon. Good seafood restaurants keep a cauldron of fish soup going and occasionally a spicy squid and tomato mixture (*kalamaraki*).

ctopus is not half so menacing once it has been nicely cut up and cooked.

Fish

The surest pleasure of dining in Greece is the seafood. Go down to the harbour to see what has been caught that day. When you see someone buying the best, find out where his restaurant is. For your personal choice of fish, the trip back to the kitchen really becomes important. Simplest is usually best: have the fish grilled. Red mullet (*barbounia*), sword fish (*xifias*), frequently served on the skewer, sole (*glossa*) and bream (*lithrini*) are among the most popular, all served with garlicky mashed potatoes (*skordalia*). In Chios, you can try flying fish (*chelidonopsaro*) as well. Sardines (*sardeles*) are best baked; mussels (*mithia*) and little whitebait (*marides*) are served fried. You'll also find a host of other Greek fish without English names.

If you enjoy your seafood stewed, try octopus (*chtapodi*), cooked in white wine together with tomatoes and potatoes; or delicious prawns (*garithes*) in white wine with *feta* cheese. The island of Skyros is particularly known for its shellfish, notably giant crab (*kanias*).

Spit-roasted gyros is without doubt one of the most popular meat dishes in the islands.

Meat

Your very first encounter with Greek meat specialities is likely to be at the *psistaria* snack bar serving *souvlaki*, garlic-marinated lamb kebabs, and *gyros*, slices of meat from spit-roasted cones of pork, veal or lamb (perhaps best known as *doner kebab*). The latter often comes with bread and salad.

The taverna may also serve *souvlaki*, along with *keftedes*, spicy lamb meat balls, a feast when minced with mint, eggs, onion, bacon and flour. *Kokoretsi* sausages of lamb tripe demand a robust stomach. Roast leg of lamb (*arni yiouvetsi*), served with pasta, is the grand Easter dish. In summer, you are more likely to find lamb chops. The Aegean has adopted Crete's speciality of braised beef with onions (*stiffado*). A grilled steak (*brizoles*) is likely to come well done unless you specify otherwise, and is not usually tender enough to risk less than medium.

Two famous casserole dishes are the test of a restaurant's quality. *Moussaka* has as many

Nibbling As You Go

When you go walking through town, even if only to window-shop, take along a bag. As you pass a market or corner grocer, how can you resist the olives, pickles, dried meat and fish, cracked wheat and every other imaginable grain? Or the nuts, beans, dried fruit (figs, raisins and apricots), *ouzo*-drenched fig cake wrapped in vine leaves, spices and chocolate? Or honey for a cup of yoghurt? Here is a short shopping list:

almonds	*amigdala*	mint	*diosmos*
apricots	*verikoka*	olives	*elies*
capers	*kapari*	peaches	*rodakina*
cracked wheat	*pligouri*	peanuts	*fistikia arapika*
dates	*chourmas*	pistachios	*fistikia eginis*
figs	*sika*	raisins	*stafida sultanina*
honey	*meli*	walnuts	*karidia*

variations as there are regions and islands, but basically it alternates successive layers of succulent aubergine (eggplant) with chopped lamb, aubergine pulp, onions and and béchamel sauce, topped with a layer of aubergine skins. A more Italianate dish known as *pastitsio* uses lamb, mutton or goat in alternating layers with macaroni, mixed variously with seasoned tomatoes, cheese and eggs, topped with a sprinkling of breadcrumbs.

Wild game is more common in the north. Try the rabbit (*kouneli*), sautéd with a lemon sauce. Braised hare in walnuts (*lagos me saltsa karithia*) is a dish for the gods, but mere mortals should also appreciate the partridge (*perdikes*) sautéd and served with pasta.

Cheeses

Cheeses here are made out of ewe's or goat's milk. *Feta* is the most popular soft cheese, **111** popping up in almost every 'Greek salad'. *Kasseri* is best eaten fresh. Among good hard cheeses are the *agrafaou* and the salty *kefalotyri*, popular on Skyros. *Kopanisti* is a buttery blue cheese found on Mykonos and Chios. *Mizithra* is a soft ewe's cheese eaten with sugar at breakfast on Alonnisos.

Desserts and Fruit

The Greeks eat their after-dinner dessert at the pastry shop (*zacharoplastia*) on the way home. Tavernas rarely have a full selection. Among the most popular desserts (all, you will notice, with honey) are: *baklava*, honey-drenched flaky pastry with walnuts and almonds; *kataifi*, shredded wheat filled with honey or syrup and chopped almonds; and the delicious *pitta me meli*, honey cake.

Galaktobouriko is a refreshing custard pie. At the dairy shop (*galaktopolio*), buy some yoghurt to mix with honey. For fruit – pomegranates, peaches, apricots, grapes and melon – the best comes from Kalymnos, Skopelos and Thassos.

Bread

One of the sweetest-smelling places in a Greek village is the bakery. If you are shopping for a picnic, get here early for the fresh *koulouria* rings of white bread sprinkled with sesame seeds. *Horiatiko* is a country bread, flat, off-white and very tasty. While you're here, treat yourself to a few *moustalevria* wine-flavoured biscuits. At the close of the day, the bakery ovens are made available for neighbours' family roasts.

Coffee

Unless you prefer instant coffee (known imaginatively here as *nes*) – which is also served (more appealingly) as a *frappé* (iced with milk) – make the effort to get the thick black Levantine brew that they do not call Turkish coffee here. *Ellinikos* is what you say for the traditional coffee served, grounds and all, from a long-handled copper or aluminium pot. To be sure of getting it freshly brewed to your liking, correctly served with a glass of iced water, add *ena varigliko* heavy and sweet, *glykivastro* sweet but boiled thinner, *ena metrio* medium, or *ena sketo* without sugar.

Wines

Greek wine had a much better reputation in the ancient world than it does now. Fermented alcoholic drinks certainly preceded Greek civilization, but it was the Greeks who turned the growing of vines into an agricultural practice. *Retsina*, the unique resinous white wine, was already a favourite of the ancient Greeks. Today, pine resin is still added in fermentation to permit longer conservation in a hot climate. It takes four, at most five minutes to acquire the taste and discover how well it goes with both seafood and lamb.

Some non-resinous whites refined enough for special occasions are *Pallini* from Attica, *Robola* of Cephalonia and *Château Carras* from Halkidiki. The Peloponnese produces the best non-resinous whites for everyday consumption.

Go easy on the reds, which are very full bodied. Among the best are Santorini's volcanic *Kaldera*, *Naoussa* from Macedonia and *Mavrodaphne* from Patras. Samos is famous for its *Samena* muscatel wine.

If you also take to aniseed-flavoured *ouzo*, neat or with ice and water, one of the finest is *Plomari* from Lesvos.

Like the resinous retsina *wine,* ouzo *tastes better in Greece than when you take it back home.*

To Help You Order ...

The following words and phrases should be of assistance when ordering food and drink. In addition, you may want to purchase a copy of the Berlitz EUROPEAN MENU READER or the Berlitz GREEK PHRASE BOOK AND DICTIONARY, both of which have a comprehensive glossary of Greek wining and dining.

Could we have a table?	**Tha boroúsame na échoume éna trapézi?**

I'd like a/an/some ...		**Tha íthela ...**	
beer	**mía bíra**	napkin	**éna trapezo-mándilo**
bread	**psomí**		
coffee	**éna kafé**	potatoes	**patátes**
cutlery	**machero-pírouna**	rice	**rízi**
		salad	**mía saláta**
dessert	**éna glikó**	sandwich	**éna sánduïts**
fish	**psári**	soup	**mía soúpa**
fruit	**froúta**	sugar	**záchari**
glass	**éna potíri**	tea	**éna tsäï**
meat	**kréas**	(iced) water	**(pagoméno) neró**
milk	**gála**		
mineral water	**metallikó neró**	wine	**krasí**

... and Read the Menu

avgó	egg	**barboúni**	red mullet
arní	lamb	**manitári**	mushrooms
vassilikos	basil	**melitsána**	aubergine
vodinó	beef	**omeléta**	omelette
garída	prawns	**pagotó**	ice-cream
kirinó	pork	**pepóni**	melon
kotópoulo	chicken	**pipéri**	peppers
kremídi	onions	**skórdo**	garlic
114 ktapódi	octopus	**tirí**	cheese

BLUEPRINT
for a
Perfect Trip

An A–Z Summary of Practical Information

Listed after many entries is an appropriate Greek translation, usually in the singular. You may find this vocabulary useful when asking for information or assistance during your stay.

A

ACCOMMODATION (See also CAMPING on p.118, YOUTH HOSTELS on p.139, and RECOMMENDED HOTELS starting on p.66)
Accommodation on the islands ranges from the rustic comfort of a room in a village to the luxury of a hotel-bungalow in a beach resort.

Hotels. If you are travelling without reservations, ask the local office of the Greek National Tourist Organization, signposted 'EOT', (see TOURIST INFORMATION OFFICES on p.136) for help. In high season, large hotels are usually fully booked by package-tour organizations, but no matter where you are, a room will usually be found for you somewhere. One solution, delightful on a warm, starry night, is 'roof-space' whereby cheaper hotels offer a mattress on their roof.

The Greek National Tourist Organization maintains a comprehensive list of hotels. The hotels are divided into 6 classes: Luxury, A, B, C, D and E. Prices for all classes other than luxury are government controlled. Rates and extra charges (such as air conditioning or television in those hotels where these are optional) must be displayed in your room. Nevertheless, to avoid unpleasant surprises with your bill, check arrangements in advance. During high season, for instance, hotel management may insist on your taking at least half board. The advantage of hotels without restaurants (Class C and down) is that you will not be pinned down by half-board obligation. In many hotels reductions can be arranged for children.

A less expensive alternative to hotels are pensions (boarding-houses), which come in three categories: A, B and C.

Private Accommodation in the islanders' own homes is a good way to get to know the people, but increasingly rooms are purpose-built in characterless modern blocks. However, away from the main resorts you can find pleasant rooms. The accepted sign to look for (in English) is 'Rent Room'. If the sign is neon, don't expect much. In some places, the rooms are administered by the local Tourist Police, who have to ensure that the hotels are filled up first. In low season, many private rooms are closed down to favour hotel business.

Villas range from small cottages to lavish summer houses, let on a monthly or even weekly basis. When booking, ascertain the complete facilities – which normally, but not always, include refrigerator, hot water and electricity, and vary regarding bed-linen and towels.

I'd like a single/double room.	**Tha íthela éna monó/dipló domátio.**
with bath/shower	**me bánio/dous**
What is the rate per night?	**Piá íne i timí giá mía níkta?**

AIRPORT (ΑΕΡΟΔΡΟΜΙΟ – *aerodrómio*)

Athens for the south and central Aegean and Thessaloniki for the north are the two main international airports. The following islands covered by this book have airports: Chios, Karpathos, Kos, Lesvos, Limnos, Mykonos, Paros, Samos, Santorini, Skiathos and Skyros. Some of them handle charter flights direct from abroad.

Members of charter or package-tour groups are shepherded through customs with a minimum of formalities, then transferred to a waiting coach to their resort hotel. For individual passengers, taxis or public and airport bus services are available to transport you into town. Airports on the bigger islands usually offer a wide range of car-hire firms and travel agency counters.

ANTIQUITIES (ΑΡΧΑΙΑ – *archéa*)
(See also ENVIRONMENTAL ISSUES on p. 125)
Since the ravages of the 19th-century robbers of tombs and temples, antiquities may be exported only with the approval of the Archaeological Council and the Greek Ministry of Culture and Science. Lawbreakers face a stiff fine and a prison sentence of up to five years. Beachcombers should not even *think* of using a metal-detector, which is totally illegal. Travellers thinking of buying an antiquity should make sure that the dealer can obtain an export permit.

B

BICYCLE and MOTORSCOOTER RENTAL
(ΕΝΟΙΚΙΑΣΕΙΣ ΠΟΔΗΛΑΤΩΝ/ΜΟΤΟΠΟΔΗΛΑΤΩΝ –
enikiásis podiláton/motopodiláton) (See DRIVING on p.122)
This is a thriving business on the bigger islands. Make sure the price includes proper insurance. Motor scooters are best used in town and on flat coastal roads – the interior is too hilly for anything but a motorbike. Remember that it is illegal to ride motorbikes during siesta hours (2-6pm) and after 11pm

C

CAMPING (ΚΑΜΠΙΓΚ – *camping*)
Only official campsites may be used. A complete list with telephone numbers is available from the Greek National Tourist Organization (see TOURIST INFORMATION OFFICES on p.136).

May we camp here?   **Boroúme na
                            kataskinósoume edó?**

CAR RENTAL (ΕΝΟΙΚΙΑΣΕΙΣ ΑΥΤΟΚΙΝΗΤΩΝ – *enikiásis
aftokiníton*) (See also DRIVING on p.122)
Local companies offer increasingly competitive – negotiable – prices compared with the fixed rates of the major international rental firms,

especially off season. Booking in advance from home, the big firms are the best bet in high season if you want to be sure of a car, as the number of vehicles available from local companies may be limited.

Deposits are often waived for credit-card holders. When renting from a local firm it is wise in such cases to pay by credit card rather than have to haggle over the amount of reimbursement from a cash deposit. Make sure of the exact nature of the insurance, third-party or complete coverage, included in or added to the quoted price. On most islands, the best vehicle to have is a four-wheel-drive.

Although the law requires an International Driving Permit for nearly all foreigners renting a car in Greece, in practice agencies accept any valid national licence that has been held at least one year.

I'd like to rent a car tomorrow.	**Tha íthela na nikiáso éna aftokínito ávrio.**
for one day/a week	**giá mía iméra/mía evdomáda**

CLIMATE and CLOTHING

The Aegean has a good climate throughout the year – slightly cooler in the north. The Cyclades and Dodecanese are becoming increasingly popular as a winter destination for tourists fleeing the cold (and the crowds). Even in the coolest months of January and February, the temperature seldom drops below 8°C (46°F). Spring is short, but beautifully green and usually with some rain in April; summers are baking hot and autumn brings more rain, in October.

NB: It's worth noting that in recent years there have been a number of heatwaves in Greece, with temperatures sometimes reaching a stifling 38°C (100°F) during July and August.

Monthly average temperatures, based on Naxos:

	J	F	M	A	M	J	J	A	S	O	N	D
max. C°	14	15	16	19	23	26	27	28	26	24	20	17
F°	57	59	61	67	73	78	81	82	78	75	68	62
min. C°	10	9	11	13	16	20	22	22	21	18	14	12
F°	50	49	51	56	61	68	72	72	69	64	58	53

Clothing (*rouchismós*). Nothing formal about the islands. A tie is seldom expected, even in the smartest restaurant, and a jacket only rarely, though hotel dining-rooms discourage shorts in the evening.

One place where decorum does matter is in a church or monastery. Women are expected to dress modestly, not too much *décolleté* or too little skirt, and men should wear shirts and trousers, not shorts.

Bring a sweater even for summer evenings and especially for trips up into the mountains, and light rainwear for visits in the spring or autumn. During the summer, a hat and sunglasses are recommended. Good sandals or 'thongs' can be purchased on the island to protect against the hot sand or rocks. One absolute must: sturdy, comfortable shoes for visits to historical sites or rambles in the mountains.

COMMUNICATIONS (See also OPENING HOURS on p.132 and TIME DIFFERENCES on p.135)

Post Office (ΤΑΧΥΔΡΟΜΕΙΟ – *tachidromío*). Post offices handle letters, stamps, parcels, cheque cashing, money orders and exchange, but not telegrams and phone calls. Stamps are also on sale at news-stands and souvenir-shops, but often at a 10 per cent surcharge.

In the larger towns, the post offices have distinctive 'ΕΛΤΑ' signs in yellow, the same colour as the letter boxes.

Normally, the post office clerk is obliged to check the contents of registered letters as well as parcels addressed to foreign destinations so, though the formality is often waived, it's best not to seal this kind of mail until 'approved'. Express special delivery service officially exists but is nowadays too uncertain to be worth the extra charge.

Telephones, Telegrams and Fax (*teléfono*; *tilegráfima*). Each major town has an office of Greece's telecommunications organization (OTE), often open daily 6am–midnight. Those in the smaller towns have shorter hours (usually 7.30am-10pm Monday-Friday). You can send telegrams or make phone calls – direct, or through an operator.

You can make a local call from phone booths on the street. Booths sporting a 'Telephone' sign in English also have international dialling with English-language instructions. In addition, phone-cards are now available from news-stands. These are by far the cheapest way to make calls abroad – your hotel will charge literally double.

Greece's telephone system is reasonably modern, but the islands' long-distance lines can get clogged during peak traffic times.

Fax communications are best handled through your hotel.

person-to-person	**prosopikí klísi**
reverse-charge (collect) call	**plirotéo apó to paralípti**
a stamp	**éna grammatósimo**
airmail	**aeroporikós**

COMPLAINTS (*parápona*) (See also POLICE on p.133)

If you really feel you have been cheated or misled, raise the matter first with the manager or proprietor of the establishment in question. If you still do not get satisfaction, take the problem to the Tourist Police (see POLICE on p.133).

CRIME (*églima*) (See also POLICE on p.133)

Traditionally crime is relatively rare on the islands, but there has been an increase in theft in major resorts like Mykonos and Rhodes. Take the common sense measures of locking up valuables, looking after your passport and watching your handbag in public

Possession of drugs is a serious matter in Greece. Make sure you have a prescription from your doctor if you'll be carrying syringes, insulin, any narcotic drugs or codeine, which is illegal in Greece.

CUSTOMS and ENTRY FORMALITIES

Visitors from EU countries only need an identity card to enter Greece. Citizens of most other countries must be in posession of a valid passport. European and North American residents are not subject to any health requirements. In case of doubt, check with Greek representatives in your own country before departure.

Duty-free allowance: as Greece is part of the European Union, free exchange of non duty-free goods for personal use is permitted between the Greek Islands and the UK and the Republic of Ireland. **121**

However, duty-free items are still subject to restrictions: check before you go. Non-EU country residents returning home may bring back the following duty-free amounts: **Australia**: 250 cigarettes **or** 250g tobacco, 1l alcohol; **Canada**: 200 cigarettes **and** 50 cigars **and** 400g tobacco; 1.1l spirits **or** wine **or** 8.5l beer; **New Zealand**: 200 cigarettes **or** 50 cigars **or** 250g tobacco, 4.5l wine **or** beer **and** 1.1l spirits; **South Africa**: 400 cigarettes **and** 50 cigars **and** 250g tobacco, 2l wine **and** 1l spirits; **USA**: 200 cigarettes **and** 100 cigars **and** 2kg tobacco, 1l wine **or** spirits.

Certain prescription drugs, including tranquillizers and headache preparations, cannot be carried into the country without a prescription or official medical document. In these drug-sensitive times, fines – even jail sentences – have been imposed on the unwary tourist.

Currency restrictions: non-residents may import up to 100,000drs and export up to 10,000drs (in denominations no larger than 5,000drs). There is no limit on the amount of foreign currency or traveller's cheques you may import or export as a tourist, though amounts in excess of $1,000 or its equivalent should be declared.

I have nothing to declare.   **Den écho na dilóso típota.**

D

DRIVING (See also CAR RENTAL on p.118)

Entering Greece. If you bring your own vehicle you need car registration papers, nationality plate or sticker, insurance (the Green Card is no longer compulsory within the European Union but comprehensive coverage is advisable) and a valid driving licence. Although the law requires an International Driving Permit for nearly all foreigners renting a car in Greece, in practice agencies accept any valid national licence (including British) that has been held at least one year.

The standard European red warning triangle is required in Greece for emergencies. Despite the laxness you may observe on the islands, it is obligatory to use seat belts, and motorbike and motorscooter drivers as well as passengers must wear crash helmets.

Driving conditions: the quality of roads varies enormously from is-land to island. Any real exploration of the interior needs four-wheel-drive. Very often, the spectacular scenery and hairpin bends make equally spectacular demands on your attention – leave the scenery for your passengers and concentrate on the bends.

Tooting the horn is the usual method of approaching blind curves. Take care of sheep on country roads and highways. On village streets, look out for pedestrians. Never mind the Greek habit of pass-ing on the right or left without warning – the non-suicidal rule re-mains: drive on the right, pass on the left.

Traffic police: patrol cars are rare but easily recognizable by the word POLICE in large letters on the doors. They are severe on speed-ing and illegal parking, and fines must be paid up on the spot.

Fuel and oil: service stations are to be found only in the larger towns. Unleaded fuel is now available in all the main resorts.

Road signs. Most road signs are the standard pictographs used throughout Europe. However, you may also meet these written signs:

ΑΔΙΕΞΟΔΟΣ	No through road
ΑΛΤ/ΣΤΟΜ	Stop
ΑΝΩΜΑΛΙΑ ΟΔΟΣΤΡΩΜΑΤΟΣ	Bad road surface
ΑΠΑΓΟΡΕΥΕΤΑΙ Η ΕΙΣΟΔΟΣ	No entry
ΑΠΑΓΟΡΕΥΕΤΑΙ Η ΣΤΑΘΜΕΥΣΙΣ	No parking
ΕΡΓΑ ΕΠΙ ΤΗΣ ΟΔΟΥ	Roadworks in progress
ΚΙΝΔΥΝΟΣ	Caution
ΜΟΝΟΔΡΟΜΟΣ	One-way traffic
ΠΑΡΑΚΑΜΠΤΗΡΙΟΣ	Diversion (detour)

Are we on the right road for ...?	**Ímaste sto sostó drómo giá ...?**
Full tank, please.	**Na to gemísete me venzíni**.
normal/super/lead-free	**aplí/soúper/amólivdos**
My car has broken down.	**Épatha mía vlávi**.
There has been an accident.	**Égine éna disteíchima**.

123

Fluid measures

Distance

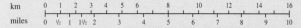

ELECTRIC CURRENT (*ilektrikó révma*)

You will find only 220-volt, 50-cycle AC on the islands. If you are likely to need a plug adaptor, it is a good idea to take your own.

an adaptor   **éna metaschimatistí**

EMBASSIES and CONSULATES (*proxenío; presvía*)

These are all located in Athens. The consulate cannot pay your bills or lend you money. Hours vary, so it's best to call beforehand:

UK: Ploutarchou 1, 106-75 Athens; tel. 01-723-6211.

Canada: Gennadiou 4, Ipsilantou, 115-21 Athens; tel. 01-723-9511.

USA: Leoforos Vas, Sofias 91, 115-21 Athens; tel. 01-721-2951.

EMERGENCIES (See also MEDICAL CARE on p.130)

Here are some important telephone numbers:

Police/Emergencies	**100**
Tourist Police	**171**
Fire	**199**

And here are a couple of words we hope you will never need to use:

Help!	**Voíthia!**
124 Fire!	**Fotiá!**

ENVIRONMENTAL ISSUES

You may be tempted to buy exotic souvenirs for you and your family on your holiday, but spare a thought for endangered plants and animals which may be threatened by your purchase. Even trade in tourist souvenirs can threaten the most endangered species.

Over 800 species of animals and plants are currently banned from international trade by CITES (Convention on International Trade in Endangered Species and Plants). These include many corals, shells, cacti, orchids and hardwoods, as well as the more obvious tigers, rhinos, spotted cats and turtles.

So think twice before you buy – it may be illegal and your souvenirs could be confiscated by Customs on your return.

For further information or a factsheet contact the following:

UK – Department of the Environment; tel. 01179 878961 (birds, reptiles and fish), or 01179 878168 (plants and mammals).

US – Fish and Wildlife Service; tel. (001) 703 358 2095; fax (001) 703 358 2281.

GUIDES and TOURS (*xenagós; periodía*)

Local tourist offices can refer you to officially recognized guides for visiting historic sites (see TOURIST INFORMATION OFFICES on p.136).

We'd like an English-speaking guide.	**Tha thélame éna xenagópoú milái in angliká.**

ISLAND-HOPPING (See also TRANSPORT on p.136)

Preparing an itinerary in this small but topographically complex country offers the logistical challenge of a military campaign.

By Air: flying is the fastest way of getting around the islands and is still relatively cheap thanks to government subsidies. Once you know where you want to go, study Olympic Airways' domestic route-map to see which connections are possible. You must correlate them to the timetable, as not all flights are daily.

By Sea: timetables of the various ferry lines do exist, available from the National Tourist Organization (see TOURIST INFORMATION OFFICES on p.136), but are by no means exhaustive or totally accurate. There are constant changes in routings and frequency of departures according to weather, demand and whims of Greek ferry operators.

ISLAND-BY-ISLAND

(Remember that this information is constantly subject to change.)

Alonissos: regular boat service from Agios Konstantinos and Volos on the mainland via Skiathos and Skopelos. Direct service to Kymi.

Amorgos: ferries from Naxos via Iraklion, Schinussa, Kufonision and Keros or via Donussa. Direct link with Astypalaea.

Andros: ferries from Rafina and Tinos.

Astypalaea: regular links with Amorgos and Kalymnos.

Chios: ferries from Piraeus, Samos, Lesvos, boats to Turkey. *Flights* to and from Athens, Mykonos, Lesvos and Samos.

Delos: motor launches from Mykonos, conditions permitting. Summer excursions from Tinos, Naxos and Paros, several times weekly.

Ios: ferries from Piraeus to Santorini and Crete stop in Ios. Frequent connections to Naxos, Santorini and Paros. One or two daily boats to Mykonos and Tinos, several weekly to Sifnos.

Kalymnos: frequent motor launch connections with Kos. Weekly north-south Dodecanese ferry stops at Kalymnos.

Karpathos: ferries from Piraeus via Crete twice weekly. Three ferries per week from Rhodes. Weekly ferry to Kasos, Crete, Santorini and Piraeus. *Flights* to and from Rhodes and Kasos.

Kos: daily ferries to Rhodes and Piraeus; daily except Monday to Kalymnos, Leros and Patmos. Excursion boats make day trips to Kalymnos, Pserimos, Patmos, Astypalaea and Nisyros. *Flights* to and from Athens, Leros, Rhodes, Samos, Thessaloniki.

Lesvos: ferry connections with Piraeus, Limnos, Chios and Turkish mainland. *Flights* to and from Athens, Iraklion, Thessaloniki, Limnos, Chios, Samos and Rhodes.

Limnos: ferry connections with Kavala (direct or via Samothraki), Kymi on Evia, Agios Konstantinos, and with Piraeus via Chios and Leros. *Flights* to and from Athens, Thessaloniki and Lesvos.

Mykonos: passenger ferries from Piraeus and Rafina. Connections with Naxos and Santorini. *Flights* to and from Athens, Santorini, Iraklion, Lesvos, Samos, Chios and Rhodes.

Naxos: ferries from Piraeus and Rafina. Summer day trips to Paros, Mykonos; Delos, Tinos, Ios and Santorini.

Paros: ferries from Piraeus and Rafina via Syros, connections to Naxos, Ios, Santorini and Crete. Trips to Delos and Mykonos. Day trips to Naxos. *Flights* to and from Athens, Heraklion and Rhodes.

Patmos: ferry connections with Piraeus, Samos, Lipsos, Leros, Kalymnos, Kos; Rhodes. Weekly north-south Dodecanese ferry. Hydrofoil service to Rhodes and Leros. Trips to Ikaria, Samos and Lipsos.

Samos: passenger ferries from Piraeus via Cyclades, boats to Chios, Patmos and Ikaria. Hydrofoils to Rhodes and Kos. Ferry service to Kusadasi, Turkey. *Flights* to and from Athens, Chios, Kos, Mykonos, Lesvos, Thessaloniki.

Samothraki: ferries from Alexandropouli on mainland; boats from Kavala stopping also at Sporades, Agios Konstantinos and Kymi.

Santorini: passenger ferries from Piraeus, continuing to Crete. Excursions to Anafi, Folegandros, Ios, Amorgos, Iraklion and Rethymnon. *Flights* to and from Athens, Iraklion, Rhodes and Mykonos.

Sifnos: ferry services from Piraeus, connections to Paros, Kimolos, Milos and Serifos. Occasional boats to Kithnos and Syros.

Skiathos: ferries from Volos, Agios Konstantinos and Kymi link Skiathos with other Sporades. Ferries to Skyros and trips to Skopelos and Alonissos. *Flights* to and from Athens and Thessaloniki.

Skopelos: daily to and from Skiathos and Alonissos on run from mainland and Evia. Hydrofoil from Volos and Agios Konstantinos. **127**

Skyros: regular boats from Kymi on Evia with bus connections from and to Athens. *Flights* to and from Athens.

Thasos: frequent passenger ferries from Kavala and Keramoti.

Tinos: ferry connection with Piraeus, Rafina and Mykonos. Day trips by motor launch to Mykonos, Delos, Naxos and Paros.

LANGUAGE (See also the USEFUL EXPRESSIONS on the cover)

You are unlikely to have much of a language problem on the islands. Many people speak some English, and road signs are written in both Greek and Roman.

There are actually two Greek languages – classical *katharévousa*, until recently the language of courts and parliaments and still used by some conservative newspapers, and *dimotikí*, the spoken, official language. This is what you are likely to hear.

The table below lists the Greek letters in their capital and small forms, followed by the letters to which they correspond in English.

A	α	a	as in b**ar**
B	β	v	
Γ	γ	g	as in **g**o*
Δ	δ	d	like **th** in **th**is
E	ε	e	as in g**e**t
Z	ζ	z	
H	η	i	like **ee** in m**ee**t
Θ	θ	th	as in **th**in
I	ι	i	like **ee** in m**ee**t
K	κ	k	
Λ	λ	l	
M	μ	m	
N	ν	n	
Ξ	ξ	x	like **ks** in than**ks**
O	o	o	as in g**o**t
Π	π	p	

P	ρ	r	
Σ	σ, ς	s	as in ki**ss**
T	τ	t	
Y	υ	i	like **ee** in m**ee**t
Φ	φ	f	
X	χ	ch	as in Scottish lo**ch**
Ψ	ψ	ps	as in ti**ps**y
O/ Ω	ω	o	as in g**o**t
OY	ου	oo	as in s**ou**p

*except before **i-** and **e-**sounds, when it's pronounced like y in yes.

You'll find the Berlitz GREEK PHRASE BOOK AND DICTIONARY covers nearly all the situations you're likely to encounter in your travels.

LOST PROPERTY

Given the general level of honesty among Greeks, the chances of recovering lost property are very good. If you have problems, call the tourist police (see POLICE on p.133).

| I've lost my wallet/handbag/ passport. | **Échasa to portofóli mou/ti tsánda mou/to diavatirio mou.** |

MEDIA

Radio and TV (*rádio; tileórasi*). Local Greek radio and TV broadcast news in English daily, but with a shortwave radio you can pick up BBC World Service and Voice of America very clearly.

Many hotels on the islands have TV lounges (unfortunately so do many tavernas and restaurants.) English-language series and films are run in the original with Greek subtitles. There is lots of football.

Newspapers and Magazines (*efimerída; periodikó*). Most foreign dailies – including the principal British newspapers and the Paris-based *International Herald Tribune* – arrive on the islands at least one day late. The major hotels are often the best place to find the news weeklies and other magazines.

MEDICAL CARE (See also EMERGENCIES on p.125)

To be on the safe side, take out health insurance back home covering the risk of illness or accident while you are on holiday. Emergency treatment in Greece is free, but you will generally get better medical care if you have insurance. British citizens are entitled to the same health cover as the Greeks, but should apply to the Department of Health and Social Security for a special form before leaving Britain.

The two main health hazards are sunburn and minor stomach upsets. Work on your tan gradually, using a strong sun-filter cream and avoiding the midday sun. Wear a hat and sunglasses. Moderation in eating and drinking will help ease you into the change of diet.

For mosquitoes in your bedroom, buy an inflammable coil called *Katól* or plug-in odourless repellents, which are very effective. If you step on a sea urchin, apply lemon juice or olive oil.

Pharmacies (ΦΑΡΜΑΚΕΙΟ – *farmakío*). These are easily recognizable by the sign of red or blue cross on a white background. You should find at least one on 24-hour duty in each major town. All pharmacies display details of local night and weekend services.

Pharmacies may not stock your personal medications, so bring a reasonable supply (but see CUSTOMS and ENTRY FORMALITIES ON p.121 for regulations concerning prescription drugs).

Where's the nearest (all-night) pharmacy?	**Pou íne to kodinótero (dianiterévon) famarkío?**
doctor/dentist	**giatró/odontogiatró**
hospital	**nosokomío**
sunstroke	**ilíasi**
upset stomach	**varistomachiá**

MONEY MATTERS (See also CUSTOMS AND ENTRY FORMALITIES on p.121 and OPENING HOURS on p.132)

Currency (*nómisma*). Greece's monetary unit is the drachma (*drachmi*, abbreviated 'drs' – in Greek, ΔΡΑΧΜΕΣ).

Coins: 5, 10, 20, 50, 100 drs.

130 *Banknotes*: 50, 100, 500, 1,000, 5,000, 10,000 drs.

Banks and exchange (ΤΡΑΠΕΖΑ – *trápeza*; ΣΥΝΑΛΛΑΓΜΑ – *sinállagma*). Although the advantage of the better exchange rate at the banks should be weighed against the tiresomeness of a long wait at their counters, the situation is improving in the main resorts, where some banks have easy-to-operate automatic exchange machines with instructions in four European languages. You may prefer paying your hotel's commission as a fee for the convenience. Note that the main post offices also provide currency exchange facilities. Always take your passport when you go to exchange money.

Credit cards and travellers cheques. Shops, banks, most hotels and many resort restaurants accept major credit cards. Traveller's cheques are best cashed at the bank or your hotel. Take your passport for identification. Another option is to use the cashpoint machines outside main banks (instructions in several languages).

I want to change some pounds/dollars.	**Thélo na alláxo merikés líres/meriká dollária.**
Do you accept credit cards/traveller's cheques?	**Pérnete pistotikí kárta/taxidiotikés epitagés?**

PLANNING YOUR BUDGET

Here are some average prices in Greek drachmas. However, due to inflation all prices must be regarded as *approximate*.

Bicycle rental. 500-1,000 drs. per day, 2,500-3,500 drs. per week.

Camping. Average prices per day: adults 350 drs, children (up to 12) 250 drs, tents 180 drs, cars 180 drs, caravans (trailers) 300 drs.

Car rental (international company, high season July-Oct). *Subaru 600* 2,500 drs. per day, 35 drs. per km, or 45,000 drs. per week with unlimited mileage. *Opel Kadett 1.2* 2,750 drs. per day, 40 drs. per km, 49,000 drs. per week with unlimited mileage. Add 18% tax. Advance reservations from home and local companies 25% cheaper.

Cigarettes. Local brands 180-350 drs. per packet of 20, foreign brands 350-450 drs.

Entertainment. Bouzouki evening, including food 5,000 drs. and up, discothéque from 1,000 drs, cinema 500-900 drs.

Hotels (double room with bath, summer season). Luxury over 15,000 drs. Class A 12,500-15,000 drs, Class B 7,500-12,5000 drs, Class C 4,000-7,500 drs, Class D 2,500-5,000 drs.

Meals and drinks. Continental breakfast 600-2,000 drs, lunch or dinner in fairly good restaurants 1,200-3,000 drs, coffee (Greek) 100-300 drs. (Nes) 300-700 drs, Greek brandy 250-500 drs, gin and tonic 500-1,000 drs, beer 350-750 drs, soft drinks 150-300 drs.

Supermarket. Bread (½kg.) 120 drs, butter (250 g.) 125 drs, 6 eggs 300 drs, feta cheese (1kg.) 350 drs, potatoes (1kg.) 80 drs, soft drinks (small bottle) 80 drs.

Sports. Sailing boat 1,000 drs. per hour. Water-skiing 1,500 drs. for 10 minutes. Windsurfing 700-1,300 drs. per hour.

OPENING HOURS

Opening hours are fitted around the siesta during the heat of the day. With the exception of a few tourist shops, everything starts closing down at 1.30pm and opens again at 4 or 5pm Noise is frowned upon during those hours. Work resumes again until 8.30pm or later.

Banks: in general 8am-2pm Monday-Friday (Friday closing time 1.30pm). In summer at least one bank remains open in larger towns 5-7pm and for short periods on Saturdays for money changing only.

Museums and Historical Sites: hours vary from year to year and town to town, so check with the local tourist information office. Closing day may be variously Sunday, Monday or Tuesday.

Post Offices: in the main towns 8am-7pm, elsewhere only until 2pm

Restaurants: lunch noon-3pm, dinner 8pm-midnight.

Shops: Shops generally open about 8.30am. Closing hours are highly unpredictable, but in some places, on Monday, Wednesday and Saturday, shops close for the day at lunchtime – opening up for evening business, roughly 5.30-8pm, only on Tuesday, Thursday and Friday. Shops catering for tourists often stay open during the siesta.

PHOTOGRAPHY (ΦΩΤΟΓΡΑΦΕΙΟ – *fotografío*)

Leading brands of film and processing are available on the islands but they are not a bargain. – it's best to bring your own supplies. Both 1- and 4-hour processing are available for about the same cost as you would pay at home, but in the smaller resorts the quality can be poor.

Hand-held photo equipment – not tripods – may be used in museums and on archaeological sites, but be prepared to pay a small fee.

For security reasons, it is illegal to use a telephoto lens aboard an aircraft over Greece, but there are no restrictions on ordinary still, ciné- and video cameras. Photography is forbidden around Athens and Thessaloniki airport and near military installations on Limnos.

For handy tips on how to get the most out of your holiday photographs, purchase a copy of the Berlitz-Nikon POCKET GUIDE TO TRAVEL PHOTOGRAPHY (available in the UK only).

I'd like some film for this camera.	**Tha íthela éna film giaftí ti michaní.**
black-and-white film	**asprómavro film**
colour film	**énchromo film**
35mm film	**éna film triánda pénde milimétr**
colour slides	**énchromo film giá sláïds**
super-8	**soúper-októ**
How long will it take to develop (and print) this film?	**Se pósses iméres boríte na emfanísete (ke na ektipósete) aftó to film?**

POLICE (See also EMERGENCIES on p.125)

There are two kinds of police. Regular policemen (*chorofílakes*) – dealing with major crimes, resident and work permits and crimes involving visitors – wear green uniforms. 'POLICE' is written on the doors of patrol cars. Their emergency telephone number is **100**.

For foreign visitors in distress, there is a separate branch of the police known as *Touristikí Astynomía* (Tourist Police). On their dark-grey uniforms they wear national-flag patches, Union Jack, etc. to indicate which foreign languages they speak. **Tourist police** have the authority to inspect prices in restaurants and hotels. If you have a complaint, these are the people to see. To get in touch with them, inquire at any tourist information office or telephone **171**.

Where's the nearest police station?	**Pou íne to kodinótero astinomikó tmíma?**

PUBLIC HOLIDAYS *(argíes)*
(See also the CALENDAR of EVENTS on p.98)
The following civil and religious holidays are observed throughout Greece with banks, offices and shops remaining closed:

1 January	*Protochoniá*	New Year's Day
6 January	*ton Theofaníon*	Epiphany
25 March	*Ikostí Pémti Martíou (tou Evangelismoú)*	Greek Independence Day
1 May	*Protomagiá*	May Day
15 August	*Dekapendávgoustos (tis Panagías)*	Assumption Day
28 October	*Ikostí Ogdóï Oktovríou*	'No' *(óchi)* Day, commemorating Greek defiance of Italian invasion in 1940
25 December	*Christoúgenna*	Christmas Day
26 December	*défteri iméra ton Christougénnon*	St Stephen's Day

Movable dates of Orthodox calendar, different from Catholic and Protestant calendars:

Katharí Deftéra	1st Day of Lent (Clean Monday)
Megalí Paraskeví	Good Friday
Deftéra tou Páscha	Easter Monday
Análipsis	Ascension
tou Agíou Pnévmatos	Whit Monday (Holy Monday)

RELIGION

The islands' faith is almost 100% Greek Orthodox. Services start around 8.30am on Sundays and feast days, and last about 2½ hours. There are a few Catholic churches, principally on Tinos, where mass is said on Saturdays, Sundays and holy days.

TIME DIFFERENCES

	New York	London	**Aegean**	Jo'burg	Sydney	Auckland
winter:	5am	10am	**noon**	noon	9pm	11pm
summer:	5am	10am	**noon**	11am	7pm	9pm

TIPPING

By law, service charges are included in the bill at hotels, restaurants and tavernas. The Greeks are not tip-greedy, but it is customary to leave a little extra – unless, of course, the service has not been good.

Hotel-porter, per bag	200-300 drs.
Waiter	5% (*optional*)
Taxi driver	10% (*optional*, but customary)
Lavatory attendant	50 drs.

TOILETS/RESTROOMS (ΤΟΥΑΛΕΤΤΕΣ – *toualéttes*)

Larger towns have public toilets, often located near the markets or in the public parks. Remember to leave a small tip if there is an attendant. In villages, try a café or taverna. If you drop in specifically to use the facilities, it is customary to have a drink before leaving. Except in modest establishments, there are generally two doors, marked ΓΥΝΑΙΚΩΝ (ladies) and ΑΝΔΡΩΝ (gentlemen).

Note: if there's a waste bin, you're expected to put toilet tissue in that – not down the toilet. Toilets easily become clogged!

TOURIST INFORMATION OFFICES
(*grafío pliforíon tourismoú*)

The following branches of the Greek National Tourist Organization can supply you with useful brochures, ferry schedules and maps in English. They will also let you consult their master directory of hotels, listing all facilities and prices.

UK: 4 Conduit Street, London W1R 0DJ; tel. 0171 734 5997.

USA: 645 5th Avenue, New York, NY 10022; tel. (212) 421 5777; 168 N. Michigan Avenue, Chicago, IL 60601; tel. (312) 782 1084; 11 W. 6th Street, Los Angeles, CA 90017; tel (213) 626 6696.

Canada: 80 Bloor Street West, Suite 1403, Toronto, Ontario M5S 2V1; tel. (416) 968 2220; 1233 rue de la Montagne, Montreal, Quebec H3G 1Z2; tel. (514) 871 1535.

On the islands, the local offices of the Greek National Tourist Organization are signposted EOT (*Ellinikós Organismós Tourismoú*). Their opening hours now tend to follow at best the example of the local shops, observing shorter hours in low season.

Where's the tourist office? **Pou íne to grafío tourismoú?**

TRANSPORT (See also ISLAND-HOPPING on p.125)

Buses (*leoforío*). Although unpredictable in their schedules, buses are at least a great adventure. Expect loud *bouzouki* music, goats, lambs and poultry as fellow passengers. To be sure of a seat, get to the bus station early – the livestock is not always polite. Fares are very reasonable, a tenth of what you might pay by taxi. Before setting off, make sure there is a return service available the same day.

Taxis (ΤΑΞΙ – *taxi*). Taxis are not cheap, usually ten times the price of a bus. Negotiate the price, rarely metered, before you set off. It is legitimate for a surcharge to be added at Easter and Christmas, as well as for luggage and night service. Rounding off the fare is the usual way of tipping, with a little extra for special services rendered.

In larger towns, they are quite plentiful, both cruising and at taxi ranks, most often near the port or the bus-station. Almost every village has at least one taxi. These rural taxis are called *agoréon*.

136

What's the fare to...	**Piá íne i timí giá...?**
bus-stop	**stásis**
single (one-way)	**apló**
return (round-trip)	**me epistrofí**

TRAVELLERS WITH DISABILITIES

The islands have not yet properly geared up their tourist facilities for assisting the disabled. Some hotels are adapting their amenities, but it is a slow process and you should inquire ahead of time about what precisely is available (see TOURIST INFORMATION OFFICES opposite).

TRAVELLING TO THE GREEK ISLANDS

The islands are accessible by road (with car-ferry), rail, sea and air. Travel agents can help you with the latest information on rates and regulations. The Greek National Tourist Organization (see TOURIST INFORMATION OFFICES opposite) has up-to-date maps and schedules.

BY AIR

Scheduled flights

Scheduled flights go to Athens or Thessaloniki. Also available are APEX and stand-by, cheaper than usual fares. Check Olympic Airways' timetables for onward flights (see ISLAND-HOPPING on p.125).

From North America, you're unlikely to find many direct flights to Athens unless you are flying from New York, Boston or Montreal. It is often worth getting a cheap flight to a major European city and going on to Greece from there.

Chartered flights and package tours

Charter flights can be the least expensive way to fly into Greece, but the tickets have restrictions which you should check before buying.

From the UK and Ireland: Prices vary enormously depending on accommodation and extras. Among the offers are 'theme' holidays such as a botanical or archaeological tour, or a sports package. Tour operators can also give details on 'Wanderer' holidays for travellers planning a walking tour, using vouchers for accommodation.

From North America: There are flight/hotel arrangements, fly/drive with a rented car thrown in, and packages featuring one or more Aegean islands as part of 'Classical Greece' tours, often including a cruise. Besides the economical charter flights arranged by clubs and associations, low-cost air travel is now available to the public at large. The least expensive is the Advance Booking Charter (ABC), which must be reserved and paid for several weeks in advance.

BY ROAD
Due to the conflicts in the former Republic of Yugoslavia, it is no longer recommended to make the journey from northern Europe to Greece by road. However, you can drive through France and Italy and catch an Italy-Greece ferry from the port of Ancona, with its direct ferries to some of the Aegean islands, or use one of the more frequent services from other Italian Adriatic ports via mainland Greece. Advance booking for ferries is recommended.

BY RAIL
Currently, the main route from Paris is via Bologna, Brindisi and Patras, including a ferry crossing in the fare. The trip takes 2 or 3 days.

Young people under 26 can buy an *Inter-Rail Card* which allows one month of unlimited 2nd-class travel on all participating European railways. Senior citizens can obtain a *Rail Europ Senior* card allowing a 50% reduction. Anyone living outside Europe and North Africa can buy a *Eurailpass* before leaving home – this permits unlimited 1st class travel on all participating European railways.

BY SEA
The main Italian Adriatic port for crossings to Greece is Brindisi, with less frequent services from Bari and Venice. However, there are also direct services to principal Aegean islands from Ancona.

During peak season, there are many sailings each week and a daily car ferry from Piraeus or Rafina (see ISLAND-HOPPING on p.125).

Luxurious cruise ships from Piraeus stop at the major islands, usually including Santorini, Patmos and Mykonos, and often Turkey as well. These cruises range in length from three days to a full week, and often serve as an excellent preliminary overview of the islands.

WATER (neró)

Tap water is almost always safe to drink. Many find that the water served in the cafés and restaurants is better than local mineral water.

a bottle of mineral water   **éna boukáli metallikó neró**

WEIGHTS AND MEASURES

For fluid and distance charts, see p.124. Greece always uses metric.

Weight

Length

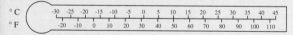

Temperature

°C	-30	-25	-20	-15	-10	-5	0	5	10	15	20	25	30	35	40	45
°F	-20	-10	0	10	20	30	40	50	60	70	80	90	100	110		

YOUTH HOSTELS (ΞΕΝΩΝ ΝΕΟΤΗΤΟΣ – xenón neótitos)

Located at popular resorts, they offer simple, clean accommodation, though often not much cheaper than 'Rent Rooms' (see ACCOMMODATION on p.116). To be safe, get an international membership card from your local Youth Hostel Association before leaving home. **139**

Index

Where there is more than one set of references, the one in **bold** refers to the main entry. Page numbers in *italic* refer to an illustration.

143

Berlitz – pack the world in your pocket!

Africa
Algeria
Kenya
Morocco
South Africa
Tunisia

Asia, Middle East
China
Egypt
Hong Kong
India
Indonesia
Japan
Jerusalem
Malaysia
Singapore
Sri Lanka
Taiwan
Thailand

Australasia
Australia
New Zealand
Sydney

Austria, Switzerland
Austrian Tyrol
Switzerland
Vienna

Belgium, The Netherlands
Amsterdam
Brussels

British Isles
Channel Islands
Dublin
Ireland
London
Scotland

Caribbean, Latin America
Bahamas
Bermuda
Cancún and Cozumel
Caribbean
French West Indies
Jamaica
Mexico
Mexico City/Acapulco

Puerto Rico
Rio de Janeiro
Southern Caribbean
Virgin Islands

Central and Eastern Europe
Budapest
Hungary
Moscow and St Petersburg
Prague

France
Brittany
Châteaux of the Loire
Côte d'Azur
Dordogne
Euro Disney Resort
France
Normandy
Paris
Provence

Germany
Berlin
Munich
Rhine Valley

Greece, Cyprus and Turkey
Athens
Corfu
Crete
Cyprus
Greek Islands
Istanbul
Rhodes
Turkey

Italy and Malta
Florence
Italy
Malta
Milan and the Lakes
Naples
Rome
Sicily
Venice

North America
Alaska Cruise Guide
Boston
California

Canada
Disneyland and the Theme Parks of Southern California
Florida
Greater Miami
Hawaii
Los Angeles
Montreal
New Orleans
New York
San Francisco
Toronto
USA
Walt Disney World and Orlando
Washington

Portugal
Algarve
Lisbon
Madeira

Scandinavia
Copenhagen
Helsinki
Oslo and Bergen
Stockholm
Sweden

Spain
Barcelona
Canary Islands
Costa Blanca
Costa Brava
Costa del Sol
Costa Dorada and Tarragona
Ibiza and Formentera
Madrid
Mallorca and Menorca
Seville

IN PREPARATION
Bali and Lombok
Bruges and Ghent
Cuba
Edinburgh
Israel
Portugal
Spain

019/508 RV